Praise

"*Mission Next* highlight~ ... ~~ leadership potential residing in our country today—a veteran population searching for its next worthwhile mission." —CPT Trevor Shirk

"A must-read for spouses of soldiers looking to become entrepreneurs. American Dream U has helped me overcome many obstacles—mostly restrictions I placed on myself—to grow my business beyond my wildest dreams. Reading this book reminded me I need to reach out and ask for help from so many who would love the opportunity to support our military community."
—Melissa Swire, Army Spouse

"This is amazing! I swear to God, it got me choked up reading it. I'm so happy for Noah! Thanks for what you are doing."
—Dino Pick

"I am so honored you did not cut out God. Everyone seems to cut Him out of the story for fear of offending others. I actually cried at the last paragraph!"
—Angela Cody-Rouget

"*Mission Next* is a real-life account of what our nation's veterans are facing as they step out of the military and back into the civilian way of life. This is a must-read for all service members who are making the transition, veterans who are currently struggling with the change of mission, and, above all, those who are in the profession of assisting our service members and veterans with this transformation."
—Jesse Yandell, Army Veteran, Retired 2016

Mission Next

Copyright © 2016 Phil Randazzo

www.AmericanDreamU.org
www.PhilRandazzo.com
www.MissionNextBook.com

Published by: Phil Randazzo

ISBN: **978-0692633847**

Cover Design: Erin Tyler

Printed in the United States of America

MISSION NEXT

An Inspirational Story

by
Phil Randazzo
with
Michael Fragnito

Dedicated with humility to those who have served
and their families

A special thanks to Dan and Babs Sullivan
of Strategic Coach

Contents

Foreword by Nick Palmisciano
Introduction
1. Second Chances
2. Today's Stranger Is Tomorrow's Friend
3. Love Changes Everything
4. Zigs and Zags
5. Luck Favors the Prepared
6. Into Action
7. The Battle Continues
8. Teamwork
9. A Morning in October
10. Good, Orderly Direction
11. Start Me Up
12. Back to Bragg
13. Outside the Wire
Epilogue
Acknowledgments
Resources
Contributors

Foreword

A lot of people ask me about transitioning from the military. They want to know what the formula is for success in the outside world and are looking for any advice they can find on bridging what at times can seem like an impossible divide between the military and the private sector. They have dreams and ambitions they passionately want to achieve, but can't seem to figure out where they need to start. The truth of the matter is that military service has already laid the foundation for success in the entrepreneurial arena. Ultimately, regardless of the dream you wish to convert to reality, entrepreneurship is the act of taking a vision and relentlessly pursuing it while knocking down any obstacle in your path, a skill we learn all too well during military service. But before you make this leap, and jump full force into what American Dream U wants to teach you, I want you to understand the reality of entrepreneurship.

It's a cold Monday morning and I'm sitting here writing a forward for a phenomenal book put together by Phil Randazzo. It's a book I'm passionate about, and I was honored to be asked for my involvement. I told Phil I was going to get this done three weeks ago, and when I said it, I meant it. And yet, I failed.

Phil asked me to write this in the middle of our holiday rush. During that time, we typically work seventeen-to-eighteen-hour days, and even though we've been in business for ten years and have many employees, when it comes to crunch time, I'm on the front lines, folding, tagging, and bagging shirts or picking and packing orders all day. A CEO in a small business wears every hat imaginable. You do whatever is necessary to ensure the customer gets taken care of and the company continues to succeed. But that isn't the only reason why I'm late.

We just went through a giant transition here at Ranger Up. My longtime friend and COO, Tom Amenta, left the company to be closer to his family. After he moved on, our new purchasing team missed some key details and double-ordered a few hundred thousand dollars' worth of product, which means we're cash-strapped right now. My stress level is through the roof as I manage this challenging situation. But that isn't the only reason why I'm late.

This past year I had the opportunity to realize a dream I've had since I was thirteen years old: I made a Hollywood movie. It started as a long shot. We were going to make a tiny B-movie. We needed to raise $325,000 in addition to the money we had already put together personally to get it done. When all was said and done, we raised $1.8 million and made an amazing comedy starring, among others, William Shatner, Sean Astin, Keith David, Danny Trejo, and Randy Couture. I found out two weeks ago that we were invited to debut our trailer at the Sundance Film Festival. Planning for the event has been fast and furious. But that isn't the only reason why I'm late.

I'm lucky enough to have an incredible wife, Suzanne, and six amazing kids. During the Christmas rush, I'm not the best dad, and I'm a worse husband. I'm gone every day from 0900 to 0300 and sometimes even longer. Now that we're in January, I'm trying to make up for it, from acting as assistant coach on my oldest son's wrestling team to light-saber fighting, Xbox playing, cooking, and just being around. Sometimes when I'm doing these things, I'm embarrassed to admit I'm thinking about inventory and Sundance, but they weigh heavily on me. Failure in either area has significant ramifications not just on me and my employees, but also on the lives of my kids. I attempt to push these work concerns until evening, after the kids are in bed. Except my one-year-old isn't feeling well and can't sleep. So I stay up until 3 a.m. with him. But that isn't the only reason why I'm late.

In fact, I can't even tell you exactly why I'm late. I've started this foreword so many times, and each time it's been different. I started talking about general business rules, motivation, and so forth, but ultimately, I want you to feel what it's like. Next week I have SHOT Show (the largest tactical show in the world), multiple meetings with important partners, a trailer launch party to throw, and then I fly directly to Park City, Utah, for Sundance. Thankfully, my parents have volunteered to watch the kids so my wife can join me for these events. We'd both prefer not to have to mix work and time together, but you don't always get what you want.

That's the life of an entrepreneur. It's incredibly hectic. It never gets easier. It tests every part of your ability. The highs are incredible. The lows are brutal.

In that way, it's very much like military life. When it sucks, it's the kind of suck that you can't really explain to people who have never lived it, but when the team pulls together to accomplish something most people would have thought impossible, there is no better feeling in the world.

And because you have experienced those highs and lows—because you have ground it out in the worst of circumstances, you're more equipped to be an entrepreneur than 99 percent of the population. Being in the military trained me to be a fighter. My business will get through our current challenges. We'll grow. We'll improve our systems so this never happens again, and there will be another high. Maybe the movie will become a big deal and business will skyrocket. If that's the case, we'll have new challenges. Maybe it won't, and we'll go back to the drawing board, and come up with our next great endeavor. We'll keep creating new things. We'll keep developing new ideas. We'll keep hiring new employees. And we'll keep fighting.

And that's what Phil Randazzo and American Dream U want to instill in you. Phil wants to take the skills you've already learned in a lifetime of service to the nation and give you the tools to take the next step. Like soldiers, entrepreneurs and business leaders are at their best when faced with a challenge. We're not happy when it's easy. When it's easy, we sit around wondering what we should do with our free time. That's when we come up with our next business idea. The hunger to build something from nothing is the insatiable desire every entrepreneur must have. If you don't have that hunger, then please stop now, because this journey will only end in pain. But, if you do have it, if you want to test every iota of your being and try to become the next great American success story, then your journey starts here.

Nick Palmisciano
Founder and President, Ranger Up
www.RangerUp.com

Introduction

I have had the pleasure and, frankly, the honor to meet with thousands of our servicemen and servicewomen over the last decade. My visits have taken me to numerous military bases across America, and each and every time I am left with a profound sense of gratitude to these men and women who have chosen to serve our country. It is humbling to realize they perform this service despite the knowledge that they place their lives in danger, and, at the very least, will be separated from their loved ones for extended periods.

However, once our soldiers leave the military, they face an uncertain future. This problem has grown as the size of our force is presently being reduced. As I write this, it is estimated that some twenty thousand soldiers will process out of the military every month—a quarter million per year for the foreseeable future. Aside from the very real challenges of reestablishing their relationships with friends and family, our soldiers are also confronted with an ever-evolving (and potentially shrinking) workforce that frequently does not recognize their unique skills. The irony is that many of our soldiers were charged with the responsibility of managing vast numbers of personnel and priceless and sophisticated equipment; yet it can be difficult for potential employers to appreciate the knowledge and qualities they developed while in the service.

Personally, I feel I have been fortunate and blessed to enjoy the freedom afforded us by this great country. While I always considered myself to be patriotic, as with so many other Americans, something reawakened in me after the attacks of September 11, 2001. I was motivated to look into joining the military, only to discover my knees and age would prohibit me from active duty. However, in the subsequent years, I took advantage of the opportunity to serve with various veterans' organizations and eventually came to see I could make a contribution by helping veterans reintegrate into the workforce.

So, eventually, American Dream U was developed for the purpose of creating educational and networking events for soldiers still on base as they prepared to process out of the military. To aid in this effort, I reached out to veterans who had successfully made this transition, and asked them to speak at our events and share their personal stories. The response has been overwhelming, as numerous companies and veterans have contributed their time and money to this cause. Our events now take place on a regular basis, and each one is attended by hundreds of soldiers. Our main goal has been to provide solid advice regarding the business opportunities that await our soldiers on the other side, but of course, we inevitably touch on the personal challenges they will confront once they return to civilian life, and that has made for some extraordinary moments. Over this period, many have asked that we find a way to reach a wider audience. The result is this book, *Mission Next.*

I began this project by interviewing more than eighty veterans who had made the transition from military life into the civilian workforce. (Audio downloads of all of these interviews are available free of charge at www.MissionNextBook.com.) Many of these people are successful entrepreneurs, while others hold top positions in government and public and private corporations. In every case, these veterans were open and honest in sharing their stories. We selected ten of these interviews to help form the basis of the fictional story of two veterans, Monica Brady and Noah Gayhles, as they confront the very real challenges of reintegrating into society and the workplace.

I am grateful to all the veterans who contributed their ideas to this book. It was my intention to create a novel that was both entertaining and educational, and it is my hope that every veteran who reads this book will be inspired and encouraged by the experience and wisdom that is shared on these pages.

Of all the many lessons I have learned from my contact with soldiers, marines, airmen, sailors, and coastguardsmen over the years, my greatest realization has been that the rewards of service far outweigh whatever effort I may make, and that the debt can never be repaid to these brave men and women.

Phil Randazzo
Founder, American Dream U
March 2016

Chapter 1

Second Chances

"Life always offers you a second chance.
It's called tomorrow."
—Anonymous

Former staff sergeant and crew chief with the 82nd Combat Aviation Brigade Monica Brady sat in her car in the parking lot of her son's school, drumming her fingers on the steering wheel and listening to a.m. radio. News and weather. Both were bad. It was raining cats and dogs, so she could barely see the doorway where Justin and his schoolmates would emerge at the close of the school day.

She was glad it was raining, though—because then the other school moms (and a very few dads) couldn't gather in the parking lot to gossip and exchange intel on the goings-on in the school, probe into one another's family lives, and generally create a grown-up version of the "recess from hell." Monica was a naturally shy and private person, so she didn't really care to have acquaintances know her business. Perhaps it was the way she had been raised, or the fact that her life wasn't neat and tidy. She was a single mom. No, worse, she was a widow. The other moms visibly recoiled at that word. It wasn't exactly a conversation starter. Besides, she dreaded the inevitable moment when one of the wispy moms asked what she did for a living.

For the past year, she had been employed by Lorson Office Cleaning Corporation, a local business with contracts to maintain office buildings throughout Essex County. She worked the night shift and was grateful for her biweekly paycheck. She expected to work her way up the ladder, but right now the truth was she was a janitor. A janitor. She cringed at the smug looks on the other moms' faces when she used that word. It had a nasty ring to it, so she avoided saying it. Instead she would make some vague reference to doing clerical work for the company, but her overalls, with the company name embroidered across the front pocket, were a dead giveaway. Regardless of how she spun it, the job title didn't feel good, particularly when the other mom was complaining about hardly having time to squeeze in her yoga class. But an officer has a sense of duty as well as pride, so she did what she had to do. She did it for her son, Justin.

When she would begin to feel sorry for herself, her father would give her that "Brady look" and say, "Be the best damn janitor you can be, girl. It's a job. Then, when you're president of the company, you'll appreciate the men and women who keep your office clean so you can sit back and think great thoughts and boss other people around!"

Her dad, Harold Brady, an army veteran, was seventy-two and suffered from emphysema, and Monica worried about him constantly. It was a strain on her mother, too, of course, who had her own health issues. However, from the day he was born, Justin was the joy of all their lives. Despite the challenges he had faced in his young life, Justin was an endlessly fun-loving, bright, healthy kid, with a brilliant smile, and a natural ability to make others laugh—so much like his father, Danny.

In fact, the only thing missing in his life—and hers—was his dad, Capt. Daniel B. Brewster, the retired US Army officer and love of her life who had passed from a cerebral hemorrhage at age thirty-eight just three years ago. And of course that was monumental to both Monica and Justin. The drumbeat of the rain on her car and the distant thunder reminded her of the night she and Danny had met.

The sky had exploded in a downpour that October night down at Bragg, just as she ran across the parking lot and into the ballroom of the Embassy Suites Hotel to attend the annual dress ball. She was going stag with a few of the women from the barracks. They knew they could look forward to a night of being hit on endlessly by the mostly male attendees, and were trying to one-up each other by inventing different ways to gracefully decline invitations to dance. It was a relief to get a respite from the realities of her day job. At that point she had already done a tour in Iraq, and loved working on the medevac team. She felt there was hardly anything more important than rescuing soldiers who had fallen on the battlefield and returning them to safe ground, despite the fact it was one of the most dangerous assignments in the army.

She smiled at the thought of her barracks roommate, Suzanne Hopkins, who had been known for her raunchy humor. She had been with her that night at the dress ball. Hopkins (variously called SueHop, SuperHop, or Hoppy by those who knew and loved her) was taken down a year later in Afghanistan. Ironically, it was SueHop who pointed out the Empty Table once they reached the ballroom. The table off to the side, near the front, with one lonely place setting, a red rose placed in a white vase in the center of a white tablecloth, and one empty chair. One empty chair to symbolize all of the brothers and sisters who had been lost, or would be lost. The two women stood close to each other, and bowed their heads as the chaplain said the invocation during the Empty Table Ceremony. At the conclusion, the entire room looked toward the table and together raised their glasses.

Later in the evening, it was Sue who elbowed her and pointed out the fact that Lieutenant Daniel Brewster was eyeing her from across the room and, she guessed, was about to deploy to their table to ask Monica to dance. Sure enough, she was right.

"Are you dancing?" he asked in a nervous and formal way that caused the women to chuckle.

"Are you asking?" Monica replied, trying to keep a straight face.

Just then the DJ popped on his next selection and the opening strains of "I Will Survive" swirled through the air and built to a crescendo. The instant Monica touched Danny's hand, she heard Gloria Gaynor say, "At first I was afraid, I was petrified," and right then and there the soundtrack to their lives was unveiled. She somehow knew she had found her soul mate, though a minute before, she would never have imagined that to be the case.

"You dance pretty good for a white boy, Lieutenant Brewster," Monica said after watching Danny make a few smooth moves that immediately made her giggle. He was your classic tall, dark, and handsome sort of guy, and looked fantastic in his dress blues, but he also had a wide, silly smile that revealed his thoughts—that Monica was just about the most beautiful woman he had ever seen.

"Well, I guess that's a compliment, but I have to admit I've never been told that before."

"Well, how many black girls have you danced with before me?"

"Probably about zero, I guess, which might be why I was so nervous about asking you."

"Nervous about me? I thought I saw you with a beautiful blonde before. What happened to her?"

"I guess the truth is she abandoned me on the battlefield, but now I'm glad she did!"

Danny and Monica had advised their superiors and become inseparable after that night. Inseparable by military standards, that is. He was deployed to Afghanistan a year or so later, and saw heavy action in the Kandahar province with the 3rd Battalion of the 319th Airborne Field Artillery Regiment. After that stint, Danny was promoted from first lieutenant to captain. As a member of the storied 82nd Airborne he was bound to go somewhere, because the unit's *raison d'être* was to be ready to be anywhere in the world within eighteen hours.

After a few years of dating, they finally decided it was time to take some leave together and tie the knot, which they did one beautiful April afternoon in 2006. The wedding was held at a waterfront hotel in Hoboken, New Jersey. They went down the Jersey Shore to Cape May for a short honeymoon, and then it was back to Fort Bragg, North Carolina, where they rented a nice little ranch house about a half hour from the base.

They were each deployed to Afghanistan at different times, and thankfully both returned unscathed. Eventually Monica was promoted to staff sergeant and crew chief, and was fully enmeshed in her duties with medevac. As part of Dustoff 35, her life was dependent upon the condition of their Black Hawk helicopter, the decisions the rest of the crew made, the action in the field, and, sometimes, the weather.

She and her crew members had an incredibly important and dangerous job. Aside from the usual transport of injured soldiers (which she compared to driving an ambulance through the air while people shot rockets at you), they would frequently enter the battlefield to remove injured soldiers. In that case, it was the responsibility of the crew chief to be the last person on at take-off, and the first off at landing. It was only when she said it was safe to fly the bird that they took off, and safe to land that they did so. In other words, her decisions were crucial to the well-being of the entire crew. When deployed to a war zone, it was a life of "hurry up and wait"—a situation could be boring for hours, and then suddenly life-threatening. A perfect prescription for post-traumatic stress disorder.

Danny had been considering extending his commission when they discovered Monica was pregnant. Because Monica was still obligated to serve another two years, they decided it would be best for Danny to resign his commission so they could be certain one of them would be home to care for the baby. And then Justin was born, and their life could not have been more perfect.

But life is what happens while you're making other plans, as she so clearly learned one Tuesday morning while at Bragg, when she received a text from someone at Danny's health club that read "Urgent. Please call." All the person could tell her was that Danny had collapsed in the sauna and had been taken to the aptly named Cape Fear Valley Medical Center. By the time she arrived, it was already too late. And just like that, her whole life had changed.

The screeching of the windshield wipers brought her back to the present, and she realized she had started to tear up. She wasn't sure if she was crying about Danny, SueHop, or the loss of her army life. Probably all three.

The army had brought out the best in her. "Duty. Honor. Country." That was something those wispy moms couldn't understand, she thought smugly. She had to kick herself.

Oh, come on, Monica, don't be so catty, she thought. *Get honest. It's not about those moms. It's about you.*

The greatest thing she had learned in the service was the importance of leadership. But now, she felt like anything but a leader. She felt like a loser. Stuck in neutral. Lost and aimless. She even sometimes found herself thinking "life isn't fair," which was just the sort of thing the military had drilled out of her. Just ask a little Afghan girl who simply wants to attend school without risking her life at the hands of the Taliban about fairness. Sure, Monica had had some tough knocks. She hadn't gotten on track since she'd left the service, and she needed a new job. But it was much more than that; she needed a new direction. She was convinced that there was something much bigger out there for her; she just didn't know what it was. After all, she had commanded groups of soldiers, and had been responsible for equipment worth millions of dollars. Her split-second decisions had saved lives. Her military experience had taught her that the world was a big, exciting place, with endless possibilities, and yet here she was dusting desks and wielding a vacuum cleaner every night.

She remembered that Danny used to say that you're just one connection away from a great opportunity, and that life was all about the people who were strangers today who would soon be your friends. And that kernel of hope was what kept pushing her on, out of her comfort zone.

That's why she was headed to the veterans' job fair at the Prudential Center in Newark that night. She felt like she was coming out of a fog and finding herself again. She had a mission, and every mission begins with preparation and then action. She was determined to find the person she had been in the military: the confident, happy, decisive Monica Brady.

Just then the school bell rang and the kids came rushing out of the building. Some of them went right for the buses that were lined up on one side of the school, and the others headed toward the parking lot, where Monica and a few dozen others were waiting. She stepped out of the car and held an umbrella above her head. Then she saw Justin, high-fiving a bunch of buddies from his fourth-grade class. As soon as he spotted her, he immediately ran over to the car.

"Mom!" He greeted her with his big, gorgeous smile, as she knelt down and kissed his chubby cheeks. She was blessed with a good kid, open and energetic, smart and playful. A real all-American boy. She was so grateful he was in her life. In many ways he was her strength.

It had taken her a while to recover from the shock of Danny's death, but now that she had turned the corner, she could see what a great blessing it had been that they had met, and that Justin was born. Justin was a blend of the two of them, but Monica loved the fact that Justin's eyes were the spitting image of Danny's. Sometimes, when she looked into Justin's eyes at a certain angle, she would feel that her husband was still with her. When she prayed, which was starting to happen more often these days, she could see all that she had to be grateful for, and it began with this little boy.

"Okay, buddy, get in before you get soaked to the skin in this rain," she advised. Once inside, Justin leaned over to kiss her. His wet hair and face brushed against hers and made her laugh.

"So, I'm going to Grandma and Grandpa's for the night?"

"Yes, which means homework gets started before dinner and finished right after. And no TV or video games unless Grandma gives you permission."

"Are they going to have mac and cheese for dinner? Please, please, please!" he begged, and looked up at her with his most beguiling smile.

"Maybe," she said, pretending not to cave in to his charms, but it was pretty evident that mac and cheese was in Justin's future. She put her hand in his wet mop of hair and tousled it. "Reach in the back seat and get the towel and dry your hair, bud." When they arrived at her parents' house, her mom was standing on the steps waiting to welcome her grandson. Of course she was going to spoil him. Monica blew her a kiss and shouted, "Thanks, Ma," as she drove away.

Just then her cell phone rang. She looked at the number and decided not to answer. It was Peter Macpherson, the army nurse who had cared for her at Womack when she'd been injured in a training exercise at Bragg. They had bonded over the fact that Monica was from New Jersey and Mac had decided to take a position at a hospital in Morristown and would be moving just a few miles from where Monica grew up once he processed out of the military. Mac was a thoughtful man who understood her situation, and had a real sense of honor. So when she said she wasn't ready to date, he didn't pressure her. She thought he might one day be a prospect, and she did plan to start dating again, but just not yet.

She reached the Prudential Center, a sparkling new arena in downtown Newark, about an hour later. It took a while to find parking. It was a crowded event—and it wasn't even five o'clock yet. *There must be a ton of vets looking for jobs,* she thought. *I'm just one of many.*

Monica wandered around for about fifteen minutes with a program in her hand, not knowing where to start; there were so many interesting booths representing retailers, public utilities, law firms, tech companies, restaurants, insurance companies, banks, the performing arts, franchises, and on and on. Eventually she turned a corner and was immediately captivated by a woman who was speaking to a group of people sitting in chairs. She stood under a sign that read "Tremendous Leadership." *That's for me,* she thought. *That's just what I want: "a tremendous life." I'll check it out.*

Monica discovered that the speaker was named Tracey Jones and had long, dark-brown hair and was fashionably dressed. She looked to be around forty or so, with a youthful glow, energetic sparkling eyes, and a ready and inviting smile. She moved quickly across the stage, engaging the audience by her manner and the power of the words she spoke. She strode back and forth, provoking a response from this side and that, and then she suddenly stopped and fixed her gaze on Monica—not just for an instant, but for several seconds. So much so, that it made Monica feel a little uncomfortable. Then, just as suddenly, she grabbed on to a new topic and turned toward a group clustered near the front of the stage. When Monica heard her say "Are you ready for a change, but don't know what to do?" she felt herself drawn in, finally settling in a seat in the second row. She felt as if she had made some sort of commitment by this simple act.

Tracey Jones spoke about her insatiable, lifelong hunger for learning, and about "formal education" versus "just education, period." Monica could agree with that. For her whole life she had loved reading and learning. She devoured books, and felt that she always learned more when she could apply the knowledge directly.

Tracey then talked about her father's influence on her life. Her father was the late Charlie "Tremendous" Jones, a famous inspirational author and businessman who had devoted his life to helping people all over the world discover how to improve their lives.

"My dad always used to say that the best way to get a better job is to do a better job," she said. "I was in lots of organizations where I knew, 'Hey, I don't think I belong here. I'd like to do something else.' But every day I gave it my all. Eventually, when the opportunity presented itself, I went on to something bigger and better. I realized that there is no perfect industry or job out there—it's what *you* bring to it." She took a deep breath and paused to make her point.

"So, think about what you bring. Your background, knowledge, and attitude. And if you don't like your job, or the company you are in, then either change the company or move on. Create your change. My father used to say that it was often the people who were born outside America who could best see all the opportunity we have here. If you don't come from a land with complete freedom, then you know how valuable it is."

Monica could relate to that. She had seen, firsthand, the impact of repressive governments, and was a little embarrassed she had forgotten how fortunate she was to have been born in America.

"So, in a way, all jobs are good jobs, even what you might consider a lousy job. Look at it from the employer's point of view," Tracey went on. "Somebody is paying you their money to provide a service. It's as simple as that. And you are free to do whatever you want, whenever you want. And if you want to do something bigger and better, that usually begins with gaining knowledge." These were words that spoke directly to Monica, the janitor.

As she stood in line to meet Tracey Jones, she felt challenged—like she had gotten a good, old-fashioned butt-kicking, which was just what she needed. She had the sense that things were about to change in her life. This feeling was odd, but it was real. She was soon about to learn that she had just taken the first step into her new life.

Chapter 2

Today's Stranger Is Tomorrow's Friend

"I have always depended upon the kindness of strangers."
—Tennessee Williams

Tracey grabbed Monica's hand warmly and said, "I'm sorry if I stared at you. I thought you were someone I served with in Bosnia, and then I realized that you were much too young to be her. But it was an odd feeling, because you look so much like her, and we were very close."

"Oh, now I understand! I thought maybe I'd done something to upset you."

Monica couldn't possibly have known that Tracey had mistaken her for the woman who had saved her life, which is why Tracey had felt an instant fondness for her.

After they chatted for a few minutes, Tracey glanced at her watch and said, "Look, I'm done here for the day and I'm starved. Do you want to grab a bite or have a cup of coffee? Do you have time?"

"Do I have time? Are you kidding?" Monica was flattered that Tracey had singled her out of the group for special attention.

"Let me call my mom to make sure it's okay with her. She's looking after my son—with my dad. I'm sure she won't mind putting him to bed."

Of course it wasn't a problem with her mother, who said, "Take your time, dear. Have a nice dinner. Justin will be fine. I'll make sure he finishes up his homework and maybe even has a couple of these cookies I've just taken out of the oven."

"Mom! You know you shouldn't . . ." She stopped herself. Justin surely deserved some dessert tonight, and her mom loved treating him. "Okay, Mom. Thanks so much. I love you."

"I love you too, sweetie."

She hung up and said, "Tracey, I know a great, classic New Jersey diner we can go to. I'll drive, and then take you back to your hotel."

"Actually, I'm driving home to Pennsylvania tonight, so I'll just follow you and drive on after we eat." Monica thought it was amazing of Tracey to be so generous with her time after what must have been a long day of travel and work.

They reconvened at the Ben Franklin Diner in West Orange and sat in a comfortable booth, ordered coffee, and mulled over the menu. They each briefly recapped their lives, and once Tracey had an idea of what Monica was dealing with, her natural instincts took over, and she got right to the point.

"Are you a leader?" she asked.

"Yes."

"Are you sure, Monica? Of course, you say you are. So would I. Frankly, everybody thinks that about themselves. But have you really asked yourself—tested yourself? Taken the risks that a leader must take to prove she is worthy of the title? It's like your rank—staff sergeant. You didn't just start to call yourself that one day, did you? That had to be earned and given to you by a higher authority."

"Well, Tracey, there's no doubt that I earned my rank. I saw combat several times, and I knew how to act with decisiveness and courage."

"Then why have you forgotten that, girl?" Tracey asked sharply, but also with kindness.

"I—I don't know. I guess it's just that life has dealt me a few blows."

"Believe me, I know all about that. My life hasn't been all plums and cherries, but nobody's is. And one other thing."

"What's that?"

"Learn how to ask for help."

"That *is* hard for me."

"Well, Monica?" She looked her straight in the eye and sat silently until Monica got her point.

"Will you help me, Tracey?"

"Of course I will. What would you like to know?"

"Can you tell me about your background? How you got to where you are today?"

"I thought you'd never ask!" Tracey replied. "I attended the Air Force Academy and received my commission and my degree in 1980. I served for twelve years on active duty and got to see the first Gulf War, was in Albania during the Bosnian conflict, and then spent time in the Middle East and Europe. It was an incredible experience.

"Then I worked in Austin for a semiconductor firm as a project manager. It was an amazing experience to be there. I'd had a great time in the military, and then I found myself in this really cool town with these smart people in a thriving industry."

"How did you make such a smooth adjustment from life in the military, Tracey?"

"I found you have to change from getting things done through power, as in the structure of the military rank, with no insubordination, to using your influence, and you have to learn to work collaboratively.

"When my father passed away, my life changed. I always knew what a powerful impact he had made on people's lives, and I thought either his work needed to continue, or I needed to end it in a way that reflected all he had done. My dad was not big on succession planning. He went full throttle until the very end. He was such a force of nature, I guess we all just presumed he would be around forever, but then he was gone. So I took over the business and became a second-generation entrepreneur."

"Was that easy?"

"Hell, no! Charlie 'Tremendous' Jones had some very big shoes. And lots of people thought I couldn't fill them. Sometimes I asked myself if I was crazy taking on something like that. Technology is changing the business of books and information at an incredible pace, so it requires knowing what to change, and what to keep the same."

"So, how did you cope?"

"Well, this was the perfect way to take everything I learned from both corporate America and my time in the military, and guess what?"

"What?"

"My military experience is the number one thing that still opens doors for me."

"Really?"

"Yep! There's just that instant respect and instant camaraderie. Somebody always knows somebody, and it has continued, even though I've been out for more than a decade. It's still the best thing I ever did, because it's just been a wonderful stepping stone."

"So, I think I have my marching orders."

"You do, girl, but let me hear you tell it back to me."

"Well, I'm going to ask for help. And I'm going to start with my brothers and sisters in the military, and I'm going to take the mindset I learned in the military and adapt it to the civilian world."

"And you're going to do that how?"

"By learning to use my influence rather than my authority."

"Great, you've got it!"

Monica smiled. She was beginning to feel some optimism for the first time in a long time. The two women sat back and relaxed, and started to talk a little more intimately. Naturally the conversation got around to men. Monica talked a bit about Danny and then described Peter Macpherson, and what a nice guy he was, and how he helped to nurse her back to health, and how Mac understood her situation and wanted to help her, and suddenly the two women just broke out laughing.

"Okay, Monica, so here's your first assignment. The next time Mac calls, pick up that phone, and go have a cup of coffee. How do you know that he isn't in need of your help?"

"I never thought of that. You could be right."

"I know I'm right! He's a man. They always need help!"

Much to Monica's surprise, Tracey said she would be calling with the name of a contact for her, someone whom she knew would be able to give her some great advice, and Monica felt the butterflies of possibility flutter in her belly.

As they were standing by the door saying their good-byes, Tracey handed Monica her business card and asked for Monica's card. Monica could feel herself blushing.

"Tracey, I don't have a card. I mean, what would it say? 'Monica Brady, Janitor'?"

"Tomorrow. To-mor-row, you hear me? You go online and order business cards, and simply say, 'Monica Brady, Entrepreneur,' on one side. Now you tell me what you are supposed to put on the other side. What feels right?"

Monica thought about it for a moment, and suddenly it hit her.

"The insignia from the 82nd!"

Tracey threw her head back, laughed out loud, and gave Monica a big hug.

Chapter 3

Love Changes Everything

"Make a wish and do the work."
—*Anonymous*

Today was the day Noah Gayhles decided to quit his job. The retired marine officer with nine years of service and a combined three tours in Afghanistan and Iraq had been home for eighteen months. Each day for the past six months he had put on a tie and driven to the office of Diamondtek, a manufacturer of electric baseboard heaters located in a Seattle suburb. He managed their scheduling department and hated every minute of it.

Noah felt isolated and found himself drinking a lot and alone—night after night. He was getting into needless quarrels with some of his coworkers, particularly his boss. He was grateful to have a decent job, because he knew many veterans who didn't have even that, but his job didn't have meaning or purpose, and the people he worked with really didn't care about the work they did. It was all about cheap and quick, and the constant pressure to generate as much profit as possible. He had identified a few minor changes that could improve the heaters, and that would increase profits by reducing customer service issues. He had made several attempts to persuade senior management to pay attention to some of his suggestions, but had hit a dead end. In fact, Marvin, his immediate supervisor and a vice president who had been at the company for years, had taken to admonishing him at the end of their weekly status meetings with the same insipid saying:

"And remember, Noah, if it ain't broke, don't fix it." This made Noah seethe.

Despite his knowledge, accomplishments, and maturity, he felt lost; his hope and energy were draining away. He didn't know what to do about it. Then fear gripped his gut. It wasn't the life-and-death fear he felt on the battlefield, but rather a sickly, gnawing fear of failure, that he would never amount to anything, that he would never know what he was supposed to do with his life. And he kept coming back around to feeling ashamed because he was just drawing a paycheck, and was becoming more and more like those people who simply did as little as they could, and spent most of their time complaining and going through the motions. Was this all there was?

He had recently started to have dreams about being in battle in the Diamondtek offices. In this recurring dream, he had an assignment to clear out each room. He would kick in the door, and neutralize the people in each room. He would wake up in a cold sweat, and it would take some time for him to realize he had been dreaming. Noah considered mentioning the dreams to his sister or his therapist, but decided to keep them to himself. He presumed that eventually they would just stop.

The dream had been playing in the background when he decided to walk away from his job, although he had no intention of quitting when he left the house that morning.

In some ways it was a sort of "take this job and shove it" moment, but, truthfully, things had been building for weeks. On this particular day, Marvin opened the staff meeting with a bad joke about how the guys who were at the top of the company couldn't find their asses even if they were staring at their GPS. As usual, all the suck-ups in the room chuckled along with the boss, but Noah broke rank and decided to speak up.

"Sorry to interrupt, Marv, but if you think these guys are doing such a bad job, why don't you tell them how to fix it and try to help the matter? Since we're taking their money, don't we have some obligation or duty to make things better?"

Marvin didn't take kindly to being challenged, particularly in front of his staff, so he turned on the sarcasm and laced into Noah. "Oh, no, folks, now army-boy is going to tell us all about our duty. Next we'll have to listen to one of his war stories!"

"Actually, Marv, I was in the marines, and—"

"Actually, Noah, I don't give a damn if you were an astronaut and went to Mars. The fact of the matter is that we're here and now, and if you don't like the way I run things, then you know where you can find the door."

Noah had a vivid image of picking up the little twerp and tossing him through the plate-glass window (which he easily could have done), but instead, he stood up, leaned across the table, and locked eyes with the man who was about to become his ex-boss. Their noses were almost touching as Marvin melted from bully to coward in an instant. "Boo!" Noah barked, which startled Marv and caused him to flip out of his chair. The room went from stunned silence to muffled laughter. Marvin turned pink, and tried to say something ruthless to save face while seated on the floor, but instead just soundlessly flapped his gums. "Hey, Marvin," Noah said while he gathered his papers, "just so you know, you never had me fooled for a second."

The nice lady who was responsible for the human resources department attempted to dissuade him from leaving, but Noah's mind was made up, so he filled out the paperwork, packed his belongings in a cardboard box, said his good-byes, and walked to his car with the ambiguous feeling that he was either out of his mind or had just made one of the best decisions of his life. Only time would tell. Once he was sitting behind his steering wheel, he realized he was shaking uncontrollably. Regardless of the circumstances, he knew for certain that his anger was starting to get out of control.

By noon, he was home with a cold six pack, sitting at the kitchen table with his laptop open. He surfed the Internet for a while, not knowing what he was looking for. He searched "veterans" and "career opportunities" and "successful vets." After a few hours a little bit of clarity came into his head and he refined his search.

He found what he was looking for—and he was surprised that he was able to get a phone number attached to a name. It was a pretty well-known name. Noah had downed a couple of beers and wanted more, but he decided to hold off for the moment. He lit a cigarette instead. He had quit smoking a few times since returning to the States, but the craving had never left him, and he'd picked up a pack when he purchased the beer.

Steeled by his boozy courage, he punched in the phone number. After just two rings, a voice answered: "Hello, Shankwitz." Noah gulped.

"Is this Frank Shankwitz, the veteran?"

"Yes, my name is Frank Shankwitz, and I'm an air force veteran."

"You mean *the* Frank Shankwitz? The Make-A-Wish guy? You picked up your own phone?"

"Yep, that's right. What can I do for you?"

Noah had reached the founder of the Make-A-Wish Foundation, the legendary charitable group who made sick and dying children's wishes come true. He had read that Shankwitz was a vet, and he figured, what the hell, maybe Shankwitz would talk to him if he didn't have anything better to do. He couldn't believe he got him on the phone on the first try! Noah had seen photos of him and pictured the tall man with a bushy mustache, cowboy hat, and infectious grin sitting with his big cowboy boots perched up on his desk. He sort of reminded Noah of John Wayne.

"Well, Mr. Shankwitz—"

"Call me Frank. What did you say your name was?"

"Noah, like the guy with the ark."

"Okay, Noah, you're not selling anything, are you?"

"No, actually, I was just calling for some advice. I've been out of the service, marines, that is, for about a year and a half, and I'm not really making a great deal of headway."

"You mean with your career?"

Noah could have answered that he wasn't making headway with his career, his love life, or his mental state, and that he was watching his bank account spiral down while the only thing that was going up was his bar tab, but he thought that might be too much to drop on a stranger. Instead he told him about his frustrations at his job that had led to his walking out that day and talked a bit about how difficult a time he'd had getting settled since leaving the marines.

"Well, yes, the job's the main thing. In fact, I quit my job today."

With that, Noah launched into a description of his time since processing out of the marines and moving back to Seattle; how he'd finally landed a job he despised, where he didn't fit in; and how things had reached a breaking point.

"So, Noah, are you calling me looking for a job?" Frank replied.

"No, not really. I think I just needed to speak with someone who's also a veteran, to get some advice. Perhaps learn about what you did after you got out, so maybe I can figure things out a little better."

"Well, Noah, I don't know that my background can be much help because my life has been more of a zig and a zag than a straight shot."

"Can you tell me about your background? When did you join the air force?"

"I went into the US Air Force right after high school in 1961 and was honorably discharged four years later. It was a great period of my life. First I was stationed in New Mexico, Montana, and Alaska. I was an air police officer and was assigned to security flights, back in the day when Strategic Air Command was guarding top-secret documents that were being flown from base to base. In late 1962, while in Montana, I was stuck at a missile site during a snowstorm, stuck there for three days, no rest and nowhere to sit, just out in the open. I almost died of exposure, but I managed to survive. My training saved me, no doubt. So, I figure there must've been a reason I survived. I'm a religious-type person and during my years of highway patrol later on another incident happened, and I often wondered why I survived that."

"I'm not feeling particularly religious at the moment," Noah confessed. "But I am a survivor."

"Each of us has to survive in our own way whatever the incident might be. When I left the air force, I went back to Arizona and took a job with Motorola, used my GI Bill, and went into technical engineering. But eventually I decided I wanted to be part of the Arizona Highway Patrol and joined in 1972. I guess I missed the military environment and the patrol is very much like that."

"How did that lead to your Make-A-Wish idea?"

"Well, I guess you'd have to say it picked me; I didn't pick it. One day I was on patrol and a drunk driver broadsided me at seventy miles an hour. I should have died. In fact, I was pronounced dead at the scene. As luck would have it, an off-duty emergency room nurse happened to come along and, using CPR, brought me back to life.

"From that time on, I figured God had something important in mind for me or he wouldn't have gone to so much trouble to keep me around. Then, in 1980, I found out what it was. It was all thanks to a little boy, Chris Greicius.

"Chris was a seven-year-old boy with leukemia, who only had a few weeks to live, and his dream was to be a highway patrol officer. I expected to meet a really sickly looking kid, but Chris was full of energy and so excited to meet us. So we made him the first honorary Arizona Highway Patrol officer, complete with his own badge and 'Smokey' hat. It made him so happy that his doctor allowed him to go home rather than back to the hospital. That little boy taught me something about the power of love, right then and there."

There was silence on the other end of the line for a few seconds, and Noah could tell that Frank was gathering himself. Clearly this was an emotional story, even though Noah guessed Frank had told it many times. Noah could feel something stirring inside as well. Though it was unrelated, he was starting to feel much better about the decision he had made that day.

"So we got a uniform made in his size," Frank continued. "Two ladies did it overnight, and then we drove several motorcycles and patrol cars, lights blazing and sirens screaming, and parked in front of his house. You can imagine how excited the kid was when he put on that uniform. I told him he was now qualified as a motorcycle officer, and that I would get him his wings. Unfortunately, on the day I picked them up, I learned Chris had relapsed and was in the hospital in a coma.

"When I got there, I could see that he was barely alive, but there was his uniform hanging right next to his bed. Just as I pinned the wings on his uniform, Chris opened his eyes. He had come out of the coma. He looked up at me and started laughing, 'Am I a motorcycle officer now?' 'Yes, you are, Chris,' I told him.

"After he died, his mom told me she believed those wings helped carry him to heaven."

Noah could feel the passion in the older man's voice, and knew he was privileged to hear such a powerful story from the very man himself.

"His family told us that Chris was going to be buried in a little town in southern Illinois and my commanders asked if I would go back with another motorcycle officer and give Chris a full police funeral. As far as the highway patrol was concerned, we had lost a fellow officer, which we had. We were joined by the Illinois State Police, the county police, and the city police. I gotta tell you, there wasn't a dry eye as we led the procession to the cemetery. Chris was buried in uniform, and his tombstone reads: 'Chris Greicius, Arizona Trooper.'

"Flying back from Illinois to Arizona I just started thinking. Well, here's this little boy, he had this wish, and we made it happen. We couldn't save his life, but that's not in our plan—that's not in our control. But we could grant his wish. Why can't we do that for other children? That's when the idea of the Make-A-Wish Foundation was born."

Noah tried to conceal the fact that tears were dripping down his cheeks, but didn't succeed. So he croaked out a question, but knew he wasn't fooling Frank.

"So how many wishes have you granted over the years?"

"Well, by my calculations, now that it's the thirty-fifth anniversary, because of this one little boy, 350,000 wishes have been granted worldwide, and a wish is granted somewhere in the world every twenty-eight minutes on average."

Noah had smoked three cigarettes during the conversation. As he stubbed a butt in the ashtray, he asked the question he most needed to ask.

"What's the message for me in all this, Frank? I don't have the means to change anyone's life, let alone my own. I'm in a transition here, leaving the Marine Corps and today my job. I'm confused, and I really don't like to admit this, but I'm scared. The truth is that I'm having a hell of a time making the transition. What did you do when you left the military, before all this good stuff about the foundation?"

Frank took a second to respond, and didn't answer the question directly, but instead said, "Can I give you my honest opinion, Noah?"

"Sure, that's why I called."

"Well, I didn't lie down and feel sorry for myself, like you seem to be doing," Frank said bluntly. "When I almost died the second time, I could have just given up and never gotten on a bike again. I was in pretty serious shape there for a while, both mentally and physically. And after the service for Chris I could have just gone back to my routine, but I listened."

"Who did you listen to?'

"My inner voice. Maybe it was God. The truth is lots of folks thought I was nuts when we started Make-A-Wish, and we had some starts and stops, but we kept on. In a way, life is like being in the battlefield. You have to adapt to change, and make some smart, quick, courageous decisions. You know that. You're a marine who has seen combat."

Noah knew that truer words had never been spoken to him.

"Thanks, Frank. I needed to hear that. And thanks for being honest with me. Do you mind if I ask one last question?"

"Shoot."

"Why did you take the time to talk with me?"

"Haven't you been listening, young man?"

Noah was chagrined, but managed to respond. "Sure, I guess you feel you owe something for being saved. Is that it?"

Frank chuckled to himself, knowing his big booming voice had made an impression. "That's right. It's one word, Noah, and one word alone: *gratitude*."

Chapter 4

Zigs and Zags

*"The role of a winner is to always be
displaying a winning attitude."*
—Colin Powell

N oah was energized after his discussion with Frank
and headed to the gym the next day to kick-start his
exercise routine. He also started to serve lunch at a
local soup kitchen every once in a while. Giving something
back didn't just make him feel good, it helped him to stop
dwelling on his problems and develop a modicum of
gratitude for all the things he had. Frank had indeed made
an impression on him.

He was starting to come out of his funk. He even got
back in contact with Leslie, the woman who'd split up with
him while he was in the service. She eventually got married
and divorced and now had a little girl.

One day, after starting to make some headway with his
exercise program, Noah stepped in a pothole while jogging
down his street and sprained his ankle. The running shoes
hit the back of the closet and he went back to hitting the
sauce, avoided the soup kitchen, and the next thing he
knew, he was in the same old rut he had been mired in
before speaking with Frank.

He soon perfected the art of moving from the couch to
the refrigerator, and convinced Leslie to do a run to the
supermarket and the liquor store from time to time.
However, she made it pretty clear their routine was getting
old.

Because Noah had a small nest egg and was getting regular disability payments from the Marine Corps, he didn't feel an urgency to jump back into the workforce. So, unfortunately, despite his encouraging discussion with Frank Shankwitz, after his injury, he started to develop what could only be described as a shitty attitude. When he made halfhearted attempts to find employment, people sensed something was off, and he continually hit brick walls. Before too long, he was regularly licking his wounds, indulging in some bad memories, and rarely venturing out on his weak ankle, except to pick up some junk food or stop off for some brews. He remembered a therapist had warned him about his tendency to isolate himself. Something the guy had said about Noah had always stuck with him: "Your mind is like enemy territory. You shouldn't go there alone."

He was fortunate to have Theresa, his older sister, who had a sixth sense about her little brother, and usually knew to call when he needed her. Though he didn't feel like talking at the moment, he picked up when he saw her name on the screen.

"How's it hangin', T.?"

"Very funny. Where have you been? I haven't heard from you in a month, and now it's been two months since you quit your job. What's going on? Have you found another job? I hope you're not just sitting around feeling sorry for yourself." Theresa had one speed—fast—and so the words came out in a jumble.

"Well, not exactly, I—"

"Don't BS me, little bro. 'Not exactly' means you don't have a job, and if I know you, you've been watching every sport known to mankind and hanging out with a frosty cold one. How right am I?"

Noah had to laugh. Nobody knew him like his sister. "I guess you sort of nailed it, T."

"Well, then, why don't you pack up the car and get your butt down here to Monterey so we can spend some time together? You can probably stand to miss a few nights of the Lithuanian Soccer League or whatever crap it is you watch, so you might as well get a change of scenery and let me help you get your head screwed on straight."

As usual Theresa had nailed her brother with the truth, and as usual she overwhelmed him with her tough love. "Well, when you put it like that, Sis, how can I say no?"

*

Frank Shankwitz had offered to make some connections for him, and so Noah decided to give him a call.

"Hi, Frank, how're you doing?"

"Fine, Noah, but what about you?"

Noah's natural instinct for exaggeration took over. "Oh, I'm great. Got several irons in the fire, been working out and helping at a local soup kitchen. Unfortunately, I hurt my ankle and got set back a bit, but things have been going pretty well in general. I'm going to visit my sister in Monterey next week, and I think you mentioned you knew a vet down there who might be willing to speak with me."

Noah didn't want to sound desperate, but he felt that way. It took a lot for him to ask the question, particularly since he felt like such a phony for putting on a happy face for Frank.

"Sure do," Frank replied, his voice a friendly kind of growl coming through the telephone. "A guy with American Dream U gave me a contact there, and I think he may be helpful to you."

He told Noah about Dino Pick, who was presently serving as the deputy city manager for the Plans and Public

Works Department in the city of Monterey, and who was a retired army officer after a career of twenty-nine years. It struck Noah as possibly just the right connection, though he couldn't be sure. But if his chance conversation with Frank was any indication, maybe he would be lucky again. Maybe he could begin to believe in luck again—or fate or chance or destiny? Maybe.

Several days later, after a long drive down the beautiful western coast, Noah found himself in Monterey. He called ahead to make an appointment with Dino, and, as with Frank, found him to be friendly and open, and he immediately agreed to clear a few hours in his schedule to meet with his fellow vet.

Dino had the countenance of an officer because indeed he was. A retired colonel, graying at the temples and fit, he greeted Noah with a broad smile. He looked into Noah's eyes as they shook hands and invited him to sit opposite him at a little round conference table by the window. The Pacific Ocean glimmered in the distance behind Colonel Pick.

It didn't take more than a few minutes for the two men to be deep in conversation. Noah laid out his situation for Dino. He tried, without much success, to keep the doubt and self-pity out of his words. But the hopelessness he felt came through as he sat in the sunlit office with a cup of black coffee in front of him. In the back of his mind, he contrasted his dark apartment with the shades drawn with the room he was in at present. He assuaged his bleak mood a bit when he remembered that he had sworn off booze and hadn't had a drink since he got to Theresa's place a few days ago. He felt a bit shaky and hoped it didn't show.

Dino sat patiently, leaning forward and listening intently with his hands cupped together. He understood, as only another soldier could, that Noah was struggling with something that was all too common. Unbeknownst to Noah, Dino had instructed his assistant to hold his calls. He didn't want Noah to feel he was interrupting his busy day. Dino knew that sometimes a battlefield doesn't always look like a battlefield, and he sensed that this young stranger was presently in the middle of his own no-man's-land. He deserved attention.

When Noah concluded, Dino reached across the table, tapped Noah's hand and said, "I'll bet I look like the sort of guy who never had a moment's doubt. Well that's not true. Like all of us, I've had my ups and downs, and I've been challenged. Many times. In retrospect I know that's good. Let me tell you a bit about my background, and I think you'll see we have some things in common.

"I've been here for about a year, retired from the army after twenty-nine years. I'm absolutely loving this second career. I never would have guessed in a million years that I would be doing this work. It just wasn't something I ever thought about, doing municipal work. Frankly it was thanks to some wonderful mentors who helped me keep an open mind as I approached retirement. But I have to admit that after twenty-nine years of being in the military I had some serious doubts about returning to civilian life. I'm glad I opened up to my mentors and listened when they discussed various options.

"So, it turns out municipal government is a lot like command in terms of the responsibility of managing a team and resources and focusing on a mission and getting after it."

"Frank said the same thing about joining the highway patrol," Noah said. He then asked, "Did you join right out of high school? College? Where were you at when you joined?"

"Well, I'm born and raised in Seattle, so I'm a Northwest kid. Went to the University of Washington right out of high school with a bunch of my pals. Joining was more like a 'hey, this will help pay my way through school' sort of thing, quite honestly, than anything else. No deep sense of patriotism at the time. I signed up for ROTC, graduated from there, commissioned and went to jump school when I was in college, and then went to ranger school after I got commissioned and took off from there.

"You know, Noah, my story really is about constantly looking at forks in the road over those twenty-nine years, with an eye toward the private sector and maybe getting back to Seattle and sort of dabbling in the business world rather than staying in the army. That happened every three or four years the whole time I was in the army. Relationships can be tough while you are serving. So I struggled with those sorts of decisions over the years. However, it was always the case that no matter how great the opportunity back in civilian life, there was some challenge, some team that I wanted to be a part of that kept me in the army.

"Lots of times I was torn, because I was separated from my wife and kids for long stretches, and believe me, that hurts. Now my kids are at college, and I'm missing them again. We spend our whole lives teaching our kids how to do without us, but nobody teaches us how to do without our kids, you know?"

"Not really. I don't have any kids. I'm not married, either." These were two things Noah felt he might have lost out on due to his military experience. "So what happened next?"

"Right out of college I went to Germany and I was in a tank battalion and went to Desert Storm. As a fairly young lieutenant, I was in combat with a really close-knit tank battalion through Desert Storm. I have to admit that was an incredible experience.

"I thought to myself, well, it can't get much better than this. I've been to the Super Bowl and I'm only a first lieutenant. Now I'll get out and go back home and pursue banking or some sort of business. My sister had gone to work in the banking sector. We're all Huskies from Seattle. I'm the oldest of three so there was always a pull to go back home. I thought about going back, but then there was this Special Forces opportunity. I was being encouraged to join, and I guess I was ready for a big challenge, so that's what I did. I went to a Green Beret unit as a military intelligence officer and spent three-and-a-half years in a Special Forces group globetrotting all over the Asian Pacific and working in Korea and Thailand. I found myself with a narcotics mission, being challenged in new ways and being part of new teams. After that assignment, I thought, this is it. I'm going to get out of here and stay in Seattle and go into business and finally get to spend some time with the wife and kids.

"But then the army called and said, 'Hey, we want to send you to Presidio of Monterey to study Arabic and make you a foreign area officer.' That touched on a lifelong interest of mine of being a Middle East scholar, and so I took them up on it. I went to DLI and studied Arabic. That was '96–'97. I went to Kuwait and started working in embassies and training coalition partners. Then, of course, an amazing spectrum of challenges opened up after 9/11 due to my particular skill set with languages and experience in the Middle East. After that, I just ran hard for about eight years— three years in Jordan, a year in Iraq, deployments to

Afghanistan. Frankly, I had an amazing time with world-class human beings."

"Yeah, I miss the caliber of guys I served with," offered Noah.

"Me too. Then I came back to DLI to eventually command here. I was back in Monterey, training the next generation of foreign area officers and guys going out to do good stuff all over the world."

Noah said, "So, you're kind of the poster boy for 'join the military and see the world,' right? You were in probably the most dangerous parts of the world for most of your career."

Dino looked down and answered matter-of-factly, "Yes, it shook out that way, but I'll tell you, something happened to all of us after 9/11, right? The human talent that focused on that part of the world—I was constantly humbled. We were all driven by this sense of national service and patriotism after the attacks. I spent a lot of time there with a lot of great people."

Noah was jonesing for a cigarette but knew he couldn't interrupt this important conversation. He focused his will and attention on the words Dino Pick was sharing with him. There was no question he was learning some valuable information, and he didn't want to miss a minute of it.

"That brings me to a question," Noah said. "A lot of the people who are transitioning out of the military right now are not twenty-nine-year veterans. They're more like me, guys with nine years or less. I don't have a resume anywhere near what you have. What would you advise someone like me to do?"

"Well, tell me a little about your background, if you don't mind, Noah."

"Sure. I had a few years of college, but dropped out because I just got bored, and my grades weren't great, and I guess I was partying too much. I had been thinking about joining the military since 9/11, and finally, in 2006 I joined the marines. After making it through Parris Island, I thought I could probably do just about anything. And it turned out I could. I saw combat in Iraq in '08, and then was part of Operation Moshtarak in 2010. I worked my way up to gunnery sergeant by the time I decided to go back to civilian life."

"That's very good progress. Why did you decide to leave?"

"The truth, Dino, is that I just wasn't prepared to be deployed again. I had been involved in some fierce action, and I felt really grateful to have come back in one piece. I saw some stuff. You know what I mean. And so, I started to get this idea that sooner or later my number was going to come up. I guess in some ways I also just craved the freedom of civilian life."

"So, do you think you made the right decision?"

"Right now? Today? Hell, no!"

"So what are you going to do about it?"

"That's what I'm trying to figure out. I'm not so sure. I do plan to go back to college and use the GI Bill."

"Absolutely, make that a priority. You know, Noah, one of the things I have noticed about vets is that we don't do a really great job of selling ourselves. We're guys, like you, who commanded large groups of soldiers and had real responsibility for life-and-death decisions, not to mention equipment valued in the millions. But out here, lots of guys, particularly younger guys, don't do a good job with that. For instance, we've been sitting here for what? A half hour? And you have yet to show me your resume. How do you know I don't have a spot for you?"

"I do have a resume, but I didn't bring it."

"Well, I guess I made my point. Why not?"

"I thought we were just going to be talking."

"Well, we are just talking, and as it so happens I don't have a spot open, but from this point on, I want you always to be selling yourself. Always have your resume with you. If I hadn't asked you, you might not have told me about your career, which is pretty damned impressive. You've done some great things in your life, and they give you a skill set that is very useful in the civilian world.

"What I suggest to our folks—and by that, I mean guys like you—is that you start by believing in yourself. Continue to be that quiet professional, humble in your abilities, but confident in your training and background. Work with mentors who have either crossed over into the private sector, or, if they have not served, understand the military and are knowledgeable about the private sector. Learn how to translate your experiences into terms that are understood by civilian employers.

"Frankly, one of the biggest challenges I see—and one that I faced myself as I made this transition—is how to speak in terms a civilian employer can understand. Things that are intuitively obvious to us don't necessarily make sense to someone who hasn't served in the military."

"Yeah," Noah agreed, "the last place I worked, I guess my military experience became something of a joke. Probably because of some of the lingo I used."

"But did you do a good job?

"Absolutely. I was on top of everything, and had made as many improvements as I could, but the culture there was pretty negative."

"But you did your best, didn't you? Why do you think that was?"

"I sure did. Well, in the Marine Corps we learned how to prioritize, and how to get a job done. Whatever the cost," Noah replied.

"Roger that," Dino said with a wink and a smile. "Most, not all, vets have a ton of self-discipline. Most don't need to be micromanaged. They obviously have been tested. They have lots of intangible skills that, in all honesty, I'm sure many civilians just don't have.

"So, I'm going to have to get to my next meeting, but I want you to send me your resume, and I plan to introduce you to my friend, Blayne, so you'll be hearing from me. And let me leave you with this. I'll tell you what I tell vets when I have the opportunity to speak with groups: I start by thanking them and I tell them the best is yet to come. You can serve your country in different ways. And remember there is a place for each of us. Reach out to friends and mentors who want to help, and keep in mind today is a new day. The country now respects vets in a way it hasn't for a long time. Perhaps it's because we were hit on our shores and the world now seems like a more dangerous place to the average American, and most folks know that they only have their freedom because a few of us choose to put our lives on the line to protect it. That's it my friend."

That sure was some mouthful, Noah thought. He had scribbled several notes as Dino was speaking, but wished he'd had a tape recorder with him so he could remember every word Dino had said.

Noah got up to leave and they shook hands. He was feeling a great sense of confidence and purpose. It felt like the old days again. It felt good to be around another soldier. Someone who understood him. When he got to the door, he instinctively turned around, pulled himself up, touched his fingertips to his forehead in a crisp salute and said, "Sir . . . Thank you, sir."

Chapter 5

Luck Favors the Prepared

"Plans are useless. Planning is everything."
—Dwight D. Eisenhower

M onica parked outside her parents' house, and took a few minutes to try to absorb all she had heard from Tracey Jones earlier that night. *Let's see. We sure did cover a lot of ground. I can't recall all that we talked about, but I sure do feel like a new woman. So what if I'm cleaning offices now? I won't always be doing that. I have a lot more to offer. I AM going to stop being so afraid to ask for help, and I AM going to reach out to help others, and I will use my network, and reach back and remember that I come from a proud tradition, and have accomplished a lot in my life. And, oh yeah, tomorrow I am going to order business cards! I AM somebody important!*

When she let herself into the house, she discovered her parents and Justin were all asleep, so she quietly went into her bedroom and sat down in the chair next to her comfortable old dresser. This was the same room she had grown up in. Justin was now using her brother's old bedroom, and had made it his own with posters of his favorite Yankees players.

Her brother, Elston (known as "El"), was married with two boys of his own, and lived in Summit, New Jersey. Monica loved it when El and Dad would take Justin and his cousins to that "big ball yard in the Bronx" (which was how El and her dad always referred to Yankee Stadium for some arcane reason). The Bradys were a Yankees family, and thank heaven Danny felt the same way. Yankees, Yankees,

Yankees. That was what he and her dad would talk about all the time. Now her son just couldn't get enough of baseball. That was another thing that made him just like his father.

She reached over to the dresser and picked up the photo of Danny and Justin. It was taken on Justin's first birthday, which she had missed because she was at Bagram Airfield en route to her final destination in Afghanistan, Forward Operating Base (FOB) Warrior in Ghazni province. The photo was placed in a frame with the glass intentionally removed. That was because she liked to run her finger over the crease that divided it in half. That crease made this particular photo unique. She had to fold it in order to fit it in her top inside pocket, which was where it had stayed during most of her time at Warrior.

Monica had been sitting with SueHop the day the photo arrived. In fact, right at that moment, Sue had been trying to cheer her up because Monica was sad about having missed Justin's first birthday. Mail call was due at two that afternoon, and Sue said she was "absolutely certain, 100 percent guaranteed, no eff'n way" the photo Danny had sent would *not* be in that week's mail; and she was right! It was inscribed: "Your boys miss you, Babe! Love, Justin and Danny."

She didn't fold the photo for another few weeks, until heading off on their first dustoff mission. In a split-second decision, she grabbed it, folded it in half, and jammed it into her pocket as the alarm was blaring and they were running to make it to the Black Hawk in less than one minute flat. She had wanted it next to her heart, just in case.

*

The next few weeks were a whirlwind of activity. Just as Tracey had predicted, her new business card was starting to open doors, and that alone made her feel better about everything. Now when one of the moms asked her what she did, she would say she had a toe in a few start-ups and hand them her card. Invariably, when they turned it over and saw the insignia for the 82nd Airborne, they would be intrigued. After talking about her military experience, Monica could see that she instantly went from "Justin's mom, the widow who works as a janitor or something like that," to "Justin's mom, the woman who was in the army and flew on helicopters rescuing injured soldiers from the battlefield."

It was interesting how a shift in her attitude had changed her outlook on everything, from work to her relationships with the other mothers at school and her neighbors. The shift had started the day she met Tracey Jones, but then, about a week later, it took a great leap forward when a package arrived from Tremendous Leadership, and enclosed was a copy of *Life Is Tremendous,* the signature book written by Tracey's father. Tracey's handwritten note said she should call after she had read the book so they could discuss it. When Monica called, Tracey's assistant put her through immediately.

"Well, Monica, it's so good to hear from you. How are you?"

"To tell you the truth, Tracey, I'm just tremendous!" This got a big laugh out of Tracey, which is what Monica suspected would happen, but the adjective did indeed describe exactly how she felt.

"I'm so glad to hear you say that. So, tell me; what's been happening?"

"Well, I got some business cards as you suggested, and found they were a real conversation starter. Then, after reading your dad's book, I decided to start living my life with more enthusiasm."

"How so? Can you give me an example?"

"Well, for instance, at work. I started to realize that I resented the very people who were paying me money, which I now realize is all on me. I would start to get annoyed when I pulled on my overalls, got to the location, took out the vacuum, and plugged it in. When I turned that around, I thought, *I'm grateful for these overalls, because I don't have to risk soiling my clothes, and isn't this a nice, powerful vacuum? It makes my work so much easier.* It's just simple stuff like that."

"Well, I can see my dad's book made an impression on you. He always said one's attitude could make the difference between something being an ordeal or an adventure, and you just described that perfectly! Are you ready to continue your adventure?"

Monica's heart skipped a beat, but instantly she replied she was ready.

"I was trying to think of someone who might be a good person for you to meet, and then last week I got a call from a friend of a friend and he mentioned that he was going to be in New York City at a convention this month, and I told him about you."

"What do you mean? What could you possibly have told him about me?"

"Relax. He's a vet who is very committed to helping other vets, and he's also an entrepreneur who created an app that helps people find transportation. The original impetus had a lot to do with people often needing designated drivers and not knowing what to do, so he knew this app could fill a need, make money, and also save lives. Unless I have the wrong Monica, you used to be in the business of saving lives, isn't that right?"

"Well, when you put it like that, I guess it's true. What's his name? Do you know when he is going to be in New York?"

Monica could hear some shuffling in the background. "Let's see. I've got it right here. Yep, his name is Joseph Kopser. He made it to lieutenant colonel and served for eighteen years. He's going to be at the Park Sheraton next week, and he is expecting a call from you."

After Monica got all of the contact information and thanked Tracey, she sat back and said a little prayer of thanks. She didn't know why Tracey had been so helpful, and there was a part of her that was naturally suspicious, but she was beginning to see that Tracey was the real deal. She was a really good person who wanted to help her. Perhaps this Joseph Kopser would turn out to be another good guy. She overcame her resistance, picked up the phone, and called him. Sure enough, he was gracious and said he would be happy to meet with her, and so they set up a time to meet at the Sheraton for lunch the following week.

Monica did her homework in preparation for the meeting and discovered that Joseph Kopser was the CEO and cofounder of a company called RideScout, a start-up that he had bootstrapped. He was a West Point and Harvard grad, who had served in Iraq and taught at West Point, and was a published author. After reading his bio, she expected he might be a spit-and-polish sort of guy, but he was anything but that when he stood up to greet her. He wore a short-sleeved Tommy Bahama shirt, jeans, a baseball cap, and a very welcoming smile.

"Hi, Monica, I'm Joseph. Nice to meet you."

"Well, it's really nice to meet you as well. Thanks for taking the time to see me."

They talked for a few minutes about the fact that Joseph was in New York to speak to a group of young entrepreneurs about developing an idea, finding capital, and taking risks. After they ordered their meal, Monica got down to business, because she could tell his time was limited.

"Mr. Kopser—"

"Please call me Joseph, Monica."

"Thanks, Joseph. I think Tracey might have explained my situation to you, and that I'm at a crossroads, so I thought it might be helpful if you could tell me a little bit about how you made the transition. I would really appreciate that."

"No problem. I'm always happy to help another vet. I've certainly gotten a lot of help over the years. In general, I try to help when I can, but when I heard you were army, and part of medevac, well, I knew I had to meet you. You guys do some of the most challenging and dangerous work."

"Dangerous, for sure, but the crazy thing is I'd have to say it was one of the happiest times of my life. I was pretty young when I went in, and so I couldn't believe how much responsibility I was given when I was still really a kid. I know you spent eighteen years and reached the rank of lieutenant colonel, and that you're a West Point grad, and then a cavalry officer. What did you do from there?"

"Well, while I was at West Point, I was primarily surrounded by aerospace engineers who wanted to go off and be army aviators. However, the army aviators I was meeting weren't quite resonating with my style compared to the infantry and cavalry officers I was meeting. So, I was one of the very few aerospace engineers who went into the cavalry, whereas everybody else branched into aviation. I loved it because I wanted to go through ranger school, airborne school, and air assault school. I wanted to experience everything the army had to offer in the truest sense of that old commercial from the '80s—the 'be all you can be' idea. I wanted to be tested as hard as possible and go through the toughest schools just to see whether or not I had it in me.

"It was a great time, and that led to my first unit in Fort Bliss, Texas, in the 3rd Armored Cavalry Regiment. That's when I met one of my most prominent, long-term mentors, Bob Cone, and also when I met my peers in the army, who became friends I still keep in touch with today, like Denny O'Neal, Mark Reeves, Chip Daniels—I could go on and on. I did the standard lieutenant assignments; I was a platoon leader and then a company commander at Fort Hood. I had a blast with that, and at the end of my time at Fort Hood, I got an offer to apply to teach at West Point.

"So then I taught at West Point. I went back and taught in the Department of Social Sciences again, stretching a completely different part of my brain. This time it was focused on American politics and policy and government. I had a nice little two-year run through Harvard, paid for by the American taxpayer, en route to teaching at West Point for those three years."

Monica realized her jaw had dropped as she listened to Joseph rattle off his history in such a matter-of-fact manner. Just then the waiter arrived with their meal and she was able to get back on track. "Why did you challenge yourself so? It doesn't seem like you took any shortcuts."

"Yeah, well there's a funny anecdote that I think explains that. Do you know anything about baseball?"

"I sure do. I grew up in a baseball family. New York Yankees. We bleed pinstripes."

"Well, that's too bad because most of us down in Texas are proud fans of the Rangers or Astros, but I'll overlook that," Joseph said with a grin and continued. "So you know that the position in baseball that's considered to be the most dangerous is third base, also known as 'the hot corner,' because those line drives come so fast; only the pitcher is closer and at more risk more often. When I played in intramural in the army, one of my biggest fears was getting nailed in the face or the shins by a screeching line drive. But I made up my mind that I had to play third base. It's where the action was, and I wanted to face my fears head on. Of course I have to admit my friends made fun of me because I wore shin guards and a mouthpiece!"

They both had to laugh at what a funny sight that must have been. Then Joseph concluded, "But the lesson I learned was to face my fears but take the necessary risk management while you're doing it."

"But then later in life, you left a secure job to start a company," Monica replied. "That sounds to me to be about as risky a thing as somebody could do. I'm thinking about whether or not I should try to start something, or just find a nice, secure job. What made you take that leap?"

"Good question. I had a great job at the University of Texas at the time, with a wonderful army assignment that was predictable, involving the university's best and brightest students. I didn't receive any kind of pay for my contribution to RideScout prior to leaving the Army. But I needed some kind of paycheck once I left the army. I'm married with three daughters, and at the time we were five people living on one army paycheck.

"So, I guess anybody crazy enough to play third base needs the same kind of crazy to leave the United States Army, with all that security and knowledge. After twenty years, I certainly knew the army, and I was pretty good at doing ROTC, but I wanted to try my hand at something new. RideScout was the way. The truth is I left the army with one month's salary. My wife knew, but I never really told her in great detail how close we came a couple of times to being hit by that proverbial line drive coming down third base. But it all worked out."

Monica flashed back to some of the conversations she and Danny used to have about money while they were living in Fayetteville and trying to scrape by on their combined salaries. "You must have a really understanding wife to take a leap of faith like that!"

"Yes, I'm lucky to have a very supportive wife. I'm the only guy in my house, so I'm completely outnumbered when it comes to a lot of stuff. But with this, we talked about it a bit—although not as much as you might think. It was something like, 'Dear, I know it's risky, and I know what we're doing is potentially going to cause a lot of hardship for the family. You've just got to trust me. You've got to trust that after everything I've learned and the people I've met, I'm not going to put our family in a position where we're caught in dire straits.' In our case, we got lucky. It worked out."

"Given how well you've done with RideScout, I'm sure it was more than just luck," Monica said.

Joseph smiled and rolled his eyes. "Well, luck favors the prepared, I'd say. That's where your military training can come in handy."

"How do you think the military helped prepare you to start a company?"

"Well, you know what it's like during a deployment. You're dealing with uncertainty every day. The start-up could be successful or implode based on the team, the focus, the mission. Sound familiar? In many ways, that is the persona, the stereotype, of the cavalry officer—to ride to the sound of guns, to pick up and move and go from one place to another, to be out in front looking for bad guys.

"I don't know what the future holds. I don't know how consumers are going to react. I don't know how reporters are going to take to our story of what we're building. In a sense, it was a simple transition because I was used to dealing with unknowns as a cavalry officer, especially when I was deployed in Iraq. I was used to dealing with ambiguity in orders coming down from above, telling me to 'just make it happen.' So in many ways it was an extreme transition, and in other ways it was familiar."

Joseph asked the waiter to bring the check, and stopped Monica when she reached for her wallet. "No, Monica. This is on me. It's my pleasure. I've had plenty of people help me along the way."

Monica was touched by Joseph's sincerity and kindness. She wanted to be more like that with others, particularly veterans. They got up to walk to the door, but lingered at the entrance and continued talking. Monica wanted to learn a little more about his company.

"Joseph, I really appreciate all of the time you've taken. I know you have to run, but I want to ask you about RideScout. It sounds like a real challenge. What keeps you so committed?"

"I truly believe in what we're doing. I'm doing what I set out to do back in May of 2011, when it was a hobby on nights and weekends. In other words, I was doing this for free. In fact, I was giving up free time, conceivably time out on the golf course and time with family, because I felt like this was something I would use. At first I was just interested in trying to build it for myself, and that's when my partner, Craig, saw it and said, 'Holy crap, we could turn that into a company.' I said, 'I don't know how to turn this into a company.' He said, 'Don't worry. I do.'

"What keeps me going is the fact that what we're doing could save lives, directly and indirectly. Directly, it gives people alternatives to driving their own cars, especially when they want to go out drinking. If we can get at the eleven thousand lives we lose each year in the US to drunk driving, I think we'll be doing something right.

"Indirectly, if we can reduce our planet's dependency on oil from the Middle East and countries hostile to the US, then we don't have to send America's sons and daughters of the military over to those parts of the world to defend oil that we pump into our tanks and burn in traffic."

"Okay, I get it. That is really something. Thanks so much, Joseph, and good luck with your company," Monica said, as they shook hands and Joseph scurried off to deliver a talk in the ballroom upstairs.

*

It was a beautiful late spring day in New York City, so Monica decided to walk to Penn Station. It reminded her of the sort of day it was on September 11, 2001, when this city was forever altered and the whole world was thrown into chaos. *Crystal clear skies and a little warmer than usual.* She ruminated on the fact that so many things had changed in her life in the last fifteen years. How far she had come, and how much she had lost. Joseph's enthusiasm and faith in the future made her reflect on the way she had been the last few years. The truth was that after Danny's death she had allowed herself to sink deeper and deeper. There were countless people who tried to pull her out of her despair, but she had stayed committed to the darkness. Anytime she would start to feel some inkling of happiness, she would stop herself because she felt she was being disloyal to Danny.

Now she was beginning to see how foolish, self-centered, and destructive she had been. She had a responsibility to Justin, to all the people who loved her, and to herself to stop wallowing in self-pity and rebuild her life.

As she approached Thirty-Fourth Street and Seventh Avenue, she noticed a man dressed in fatigues who looked to be around fifty or so, but was probably closer to her age. He was grimy, sweaty, smelly, and sitting on the pavement in what appeared to be a puddle of urine, leaning against the gleaming front window of a computer store that popped and fizzled with the latest electronic toys. His left leg was amputated below the knee, and the little basket in front of him contained a few dollars and some change. People stepped around him, annoyed at the disruption. Monica couldn't help but be repulsed. He displayed a cardboard sign that read "Afghanistan Vet. Please help." As she hurried past, his voice pierced the din, and she clearly heard his sing-song as if he were speaking solely to her. He repeated his simple appeal over and over: "Please help *Me!*"

She turned her head in disgust and wove her way through the throng, determined to beat the crowd that was pouring down the stairs at Penn Station. *That poor guy. I guess I should have given him a dollar or at least my spare change. Too late now. My train leaves in five minutes and I have to pick up Justin at school. There really isn't anything I can do for him, anyway.*

At the bottom of the stairs she abruptly reversed course and pushed her way back up the steps, despite the protests of the other commuters. His cry had chased her down the street, dug its claws into her, and wouldn't let go. It dawned on her that this man and this place were just an extension of the battlefields she and her crew had landed in, the chopper whirring and chucking and blowing up the dust, until she would finally spot the injured soldier across the field pleading for help. She never quite knew what awaited her back then, and she didn't know what was going to happen now. But she knew she could not abandon a fellow soldier.

Chapter 6

Into Action

*"Service to others is the rent you pay
for your room here on earth."*
—Muhammad Ali

N oah was bursting with enthusiasm when he returned to Theresa's house. He found her out in the backyard playing with her beloved dog, Toby, a rescue who had started life in Puerto Rico and, miraculously and improbably, somehow made his way to her home in Monterey. She always said Toby was proof that one should never give up.

One day she had unexpectedly received a call from a veterinarian friend who was, at that moment, standing at a place known as "Dead Dog Beach" in Puerto Rico. He was holding a five-week-old Rottweiler-Dachshund mix who was the only pup saved from a litter, and whose fate was either to be put on a plane and flown to California (ultimately to wind up with Theresa), or to be tossed in the water to drown. Despite the fact that until that instant, Theresa had absolutely no intention of owning a dog, she immediately said, "Don't let him die. I'll take him." It turned out to be a spontaneous decision with monumental results.

The truth was that Theresa, twice-divorced and in a bad way at the time, had known she could use the company. And Toby turned out to be the right move in more ways than one. Not only did they immediately bond like two shipwrecked survivors clinging to a life preserver, but it turned out that Toby was literally just what the doctor had ordered. At her last checkup, Theresa's doctor had told her she'd better do something about her weight soon, or they'd be fitting her for new knees. Toby turned out to be her "personal trainer," as she now jokingly referred to him. At the point he came into her life, she had eaten herself into a 2X dress size. She pretended she was around 240 pounds, but actually tipped the scales at around 250. At first, the duo started walking, and Theresa could only manage a few miles. Less than two years later, she was competing in marathons, had a new wardrobe, and had dropped almost a hundred pounds—all thanks to Toby. She was fond of saying that he had rescued her, not the other way around.

"Hey, T.," Noah said to her, "you'll never guess what happened. Dino Pick turned out to be this incredible guy. He spent around two hours with me, and gave me some great advice. And, I don't know, I just feel different now."

"Yeah, I've seen him on TV. He always seems like he has things under control when all hell is breaking loose. What'd he say to you?"

"Well, he had lots of good, solid information, but the bottom line is that he pretty much said the same sorts of things you've been saying, but hearing it from another military guy just made an impression on me. I guess it's harder to bullshit someone of his stature. He sort of called me on my game."

"Well, I'm glad to hear that. But what are you actually planning to do now that you are all pumped up?"

"So, for one thing, I'm gonna cut way back on my drinking, and I'm planning to get back into running again. Damn! I wish I had brought my running shoes." He pictured his Nikes leaning up against the back wall of his closet. "I guess I can get started when I get back to Seattle."

"I thought you said you were going to cut out the BS? You think those are the only running shoes that will fit your damn feet in the whole Pacific Northwest? I've got news for you: you left some running shoes here a few years ago. They're out in the garage. I just saw them not that long ago when I was cleaning up and I kept them for just such an occasion. They're up on the shelf near the camping stuff, so just go get them. We'll dust them off and the three of us can go out for a run. Toby and I were just talking about doing our usual five miles, so the two of us are gonna get you out there and we'll whip your sorry ass into shape! Let's get changed, little bro; there's no time like the present."

Once again Noah was left speechless by his sister. She knew his tendencies. One of her nicknames for him was the Master Procrastinator, so she wasn't going to let him slip out of running so quickly. As it turned out, he decided to stay in Monterey for another week, and by the time he headed back up the coast, he had gotten into a regular routine and felt in great shape. His weight was just about back to where it had been when he left the marines, but the greatest change was in his head. Those negative thoughts were starting to go away and he was ready to begin anew.

He heard his phone buzz and noticed he had an e-mail. When he pulled over to a rest stop, he discovered it was from Dino Pick.

To: Noah Gayhles; Blayne Smith

From: Dino Pick

Subject: Introductions

Noah, meet Blayne; Blayne, meet Noah.

Blayne, Noah is a vet (marines) who was in my office a few weeks ago. He's been out for a couple of years, and is having a little trouble getting readjusted. So, I thought of you and

Team RWB. He lives in the Seattle area, and I know you've got a chapter up there, but I thought it might do him some good to have a chat with you directly. At any rate, here he is, and thanks for doing all the good work you do. His contact info is attached.

Noah, Blayne is located in Tampa, so perhaps you guys can do a Skype call or at least a phone call. Good luck, soldier.

DP

How cool is that? Noah thought. *Dino hardly knows me, and yet he followed through to hook me up with someone. That's something I have to get better at: following up on my promises.* After loading up on some junk food and taking a bio break, he sat down in his car and responded to the e-mail.

To: Dino Pick; Blayne Smith

From: Noah Gayhles

Subject: Re: Introductions

Dino, thanks very much for the introduction.

Blayne, please let me know when you have some time to speak, and we can set up a Skype call if that works for you.

Thanks to both of you,

Noah

About an hour later, while he was cruising up the Pacific Coast Highway, his phone rang. He didn't recognize the number, but picked it up on his Bluetooth.

"Hi, this is Noah."

"Hey, Noah, this is Blayne Smith. I'm following up on Dino's e-mail."

"Hey, Blayne, that's really nice. I appreciate it. I'm in my car driving home, so I haven't had a chance yet to research your organization. I guess you're involved with connecting vets to one another."

"Well, that's just one of the things we do, but it would probably make the most sense if you checked out our site, and then we can set up a Skype call for later in the week. My website is teamrwb.org, which stands for Red, White, and Blue, and we have a chapter up in the Seattle-Tacoma area. That will answer a lot of your questions, but I'd like to chat personally, so we can learn more about each other and you can fill me in on what's going on with you."

"That sounds great; I'll do that. Dino's an incredible guy, isn't he?"

"Yeah, he's absolutely amazing. The things that guy has done and the places he's been are beyond belief, and now he is totally committed to helping our guys move back into civilian life. He's a real brother."

"He sure is! Okay, Blayne, I'll get back in touch later today."

When Noah arrived home, he immediately went to the Team RWB site, and learned all about the incredible things the organization was doing to try to reconnect vets. It looked like just the sort of group he needed, but a part of him just wanted to chill by himself, which he did once he found his usual spot on the couch. But instead of vegging in front of the TV, he debated whether he should open up a beer or go for a run. He thought about Dino, Blayne, Frank, and T. He knew what T. would say if she were standing there and it made him laugh. Then a commercial came on for the Wounded Warrior Project. There was a piece about this one guy who lost an arm, but was now playing in a recreational hockey league. *Okay, asshole, do you get the message?* That got him off the couch and out the door.

The sun was just starting to set and sparkled on the lake his running path encircled. *Running is a great way to clear the mind and let the positive thoughts drive out the negative ones,* he told himself. He knew he had some issues, because these dark thoughts kept coming back. He sometimes had vivid nightmares, but nothing too severe—not like some other guys he knew. But there was stuff back there, stuff he didn't want to think about, and some guilt about what he had done in the name of service to his country. His mind flashed on the face of an Afghan woman, but he was quick to push it away. *Not that. Don't go there,* he instructed himself. *Civilians think they know about war, and they're well-intentioned, but they don't really understand. Only other soldiers truly understand. Guys like Frank, Dino, and Blayne get it.* He looked out over the lake; it had turned an orange hue. The last rays of sunlight danced majestically along the water. It was a beautiful sight. *Here I am, back home, safe and sound, with lots of people who want to help me. All parts intact. All I have to do is make a little effort.* He was reminded of the last word Frank had left him with at the end of their first conversation: *gratitude.*

He knew what he had to do. When he got home, he sent an e-mail to Blayne to set a time for a call. Yet he was bothered by the fact that, despite the efforts on the part of these strangers to help him, he somewhat resented the help and had to force himself to follow through. *What's wrong with you dude?* he asked himself. A reasonable question to which he didn't have an answer.

*

Noah reached Blayne via Skype a few days later, and he looked pretty much as he did on the video on his site. He still had a military countenance about him: he was clean shaven with a military cut. He looked to have the body of a runner, and exuded a natural sincerity that immediately put Noah at ease.

After Noah told Blayne about his most recent journeys, and his recent struggles, he asked Blayne to give him a little background about himself. Blayne explained that he left the military in '09, and was a West Point grad and a former Special Forces officer with tours in both Iraq and Afghanistan. He was now living in Tampa and was executive director of Team RWB.

"So, what did you do right after you left the military? Did you know what you wanted to do? Where was your head at?"

"No, I didn't know what I wanted to do. I felt like I was ready to exit the military because I'd done all the things I'd joined the military to do.

"When you look at an officer's career, most of the really 'fun' stuff is in the front half. Then, on the back half, there are some good assignments and some things you can do, but it's civil things, a lot of staff assignments.

"For me personally, it didn't feel like the path I wanted to take. I'd had a good army career to that point. I just was ready to move on and try the private sector, and see what else was out there."

Noah could relate to that. "Yeah, I guess that's sort of where I'm at now. But you had a really good gig in the army. I didn't see a lot of growth for me when I left."

"Well, I felt a little constrained, too, to be honest. I felt like in the army, I was bumping up against a ceiling. I don't mean that in an arrogant way, but you're very constrained by your environment, in terms of what you can do and how innovative you can be, and how fast you can grow. It's just that the military isn't built that way.

"I knew it was time to move on, but I didn't really know what I wanted to do, which was scary. I wished every night that something would compel me or draw me out, but nothing really did, to be honest."

"That's exactly where I'm at now. I took a job at a place that manufactured electric wall-heating units, and everybody ran around like getting these things out the door was the most important thing in the world, but I couldn't get excited about it. It wasn't for me. So what did you do then?"

"I prepared. I studied up. I read a lot of things. I talked to the recruiter, headhunter types, the JMO people. I tried to educate myself on the private sector. What was sales and marketing all about? What were operations about? I checked out different industries.

"I made the decision that I didn't want to go into government work or defense contracting. Not necessarily because I didn't want to do it, but because I had an itch to get into the private sector. I felt like I had to scratch that itch.

"I knew that if I went straight from the army into a government job or a defense contracting job, I would wonder if I should have gone into the private sector. For me, it was important to make a clean break. Because I still had my clearance, I could have considered the FBI or other intelligence units. But I wound up taking a job as a sales territory manager for a medical diagnostics company. It was a nice place, and good pay, but I knew I needed to do something a little more meaningful with my life, which is how I eventually wound up here."

"Well, it sounds like you had some pretty good options in front of you," Noah said. "But I still need to get my undergrad degree, and I don't see much I can do with being a gunnery sergeant." Noah thought, *Now this guy is going to think I'm a loser.* But instead, Blayne was considerate and encouraging.

"Well, you're in the same spot as the vast majority of men and women who get out of the service. You need to focus on education, put your GI Bill to work for you, and take the time to figure out where you fit in. You earned that, man."

"You know, you're right, Blayne. It's pretty incredible that we're able to get paid while we're going to school, and our cost of education is covered, books and everything."

"Yep. It's pretty amazing. Talk to some civilian folks who have massive college debt, and you'll realize how lucky we are."

"That's true. I guess I have to get serious about that. I just haven't had the time lately." *T. would call me out on that one for sure,* Noah thought.

Blayne saw right through him, too, but responded more kindly than his sister would have. "We don't say that around here. We say, 'I didn't make it a priority.' That's not judgmental. That's empowering. You can say confidently, 'Well, no, I didn't get that done today because I didn't make it a priority.' That's okay, right?"

"I'd have to say that's more truthful. I actually have the time; I just haven't made college a priority."

"So, why do you think that is? I'm not judging you, because by nature, I'm a bit of a procrastinator. I'm one of those people who does his best work under the gun. If the project isn't due for two months, I'm probably not going to start it right now. I'll wait until I'm closer."

"That's definitely my MO as well, but since I've gotten out, I've fallen into some bad habits."

"Like what sorts of things, if you don't mind my asking?"

"No, not really. I guess you would have to say my biggest problem is inertia."

"You mean you get started, but don't follow through?"

"That, and also, I just can't make up my mind. I don't have the discipline I had in the military."

"That's a pretty common issue as people are transitioning out of the military. You get used to showing up for formation at five thirty in the morning, and there are consequences if you're late. Then, all of a sudden, back in civilian life all of that goes away." Blayne had heard the same story many times. "To be honest with you, Noah, it's easy to slip into some bad habits—drugs, alcohol, and other stuff. I see it all the time."

"Well, there's some of that, too. Booze, mainly." Noah didn't quite know why he was being so honest with a complete stranger, but something in Blayne's character made Noah feel he could open up with him.

"You should check us out in your area. You'll meet people who've gone through the same sort of transition, and gotten through it. It's not the end of the world. It just takes some effort."

"I plan to check it out. I think there's an event coming up soon, and it looks interesting. Can you tell me a little more? How did you get involved?"

"I was working on my MBA. I had the sales job, but I really didn't know what I was going to do. Then I started volunteering and became a part of Team Red, White & Blue. Mike, the guy who founded it, is a good friend of mine. We chatted about it. One day, I think it was in November 2011, he said, 'You know, this thing is really getting traction here. If we're going to realize our potential, someone is going to have to quit his job and run it full time. I think you'd be a good guy to do it if you could walk away from the money and give it a shot.'

"I was surprised at how quickly I said, 'Yeah, man. Let's talk about that.' I didn't hesitate. A few months later it looked like we had enough financial capital to hire somebody. He asked me to do it and I said, 'Okay, let's do it.'"

"So, I guess it's worked out for you. It looks like it's grown. How many members are there now?"

"Well, it's growing all the time, but right now, we've got over 88,000 members and we're in 181 communities at last count."

"Wow, that's incredible."

"Yeah, the key is having something of value. We don't just want a bunch of guys sitting around telling old war stories and drinking beer; we want them to get involved with one another. You know, to try to offer value to each other and the community. It seems to be working. That's one of the things we talk about all the time—that if people aren't coming to your events, you should make them more awesome. You can't just drape yourself in the flag and say, 'Hey, we're a good cause; you should come out.'

"Eventually people are going to run out of motivation for that. You've got to make it a valuable opportunity for them. What are you doing? Is it fun? Does it feel fulfilling? Are you making a difference in your community? What's drawing people out? We try to identify those things that really make people come out and do those things."

Noah was starting to get excited about getting involved. "You guys must be doing something right to be reaching so many people. I guess with so many men and women getting processed out, there's a real need."

"There's an incredible need. And you're right. For us, it's really about value and scalability. That's what I work on every single day. That's why our staff is only nine people but we're able to still make it go. Which reminds me, I have to get to a staff meeting in a few minutes."

"No problem, Blayne. I really appreciate you taking the time, and I'm going to head to the next RWB event in Seattle."

"I'm glad to hear that, and maybe one day we'll meet in person. Good speaking with you, Noah, and good luck."

"Thanks, and the same to you."

*

The next day Noah did something he hadn't done in a long time. He set his alarm for 7 a.m., threw his feet over the side of the bed, and began his day early. He decided it was time to do something with all the information he had gleaned from speaking with Frank, Dino, and Blayne. He had spoken with three rather incredible men. While none of them had judged him, all three had been honest and called him out on his litany of excuses. He knew a call to action when he heard it. Now he had to have the courage to *take* the right actions. But he wasn't sure what he should do.

Obviously he had been dragging his heels about going back to school, and he was, at best, inconsistent with health matters. Yes, he had started running again over the last few weeks, but, if he was true to form, he knew how that would go once the weather turned bad. He was also smoking a pack a day, and now that he was running, he could feel it in his lungs. And, if he was to be completely honest with himself, he was waking up with a hangover every few days, particularly on the weekends. After returning from the military, he had started hanging around with his old high school friends, and they spent most of their time doing the same stuff they had done as teenagers. His drinking had gotten progressively worse over the months, and now it was starting to take a toll. He wasn't ready to stop entirely, but he knew he had to get it in check. He just didn't know how.

The truth was that, when he was in the marines, if he went out with a few buddies and got blitzed, he still had to show up for work when he was on duty. But now, without a job, or school, he was never on duty, so he had created the opportunity to drift. And Leslie had sort of drifted out of his life as well. He made it appear to be a mutual decision, but there was no doubt he had engineered the "sort-of breakup." When he'd told Theresa about the situation with Leslie, her response had been immediate: "Who the hell are you hiding out from?"

The bottom line was he knew he needed to make a change, or several changes. He had a lot of balls in the air, but Blayne had given him good advice when he told him to get clear about which issues he needed to make a priority.

He looked in the mirror as he was lacing up his running shoes and said out loud, "Just quit the bullshit, Noah." He had to laugh, because he had also noticed that, with his increasing isolation, he was talking to himself more and more. That made him think of Enrique Rios, his best buddy from the marines. They had bonded when they discovered they were both from the state of Washington and big Seahawks fans. And because they deployed together, they shared a lot of time in Afghanistan. When you live in such close quarters, it's hard to hide your quirks—like talking to people who aren't present. He remembered one time when Rios was lying on his bunk, trying to catch some z's, and Noah was replaying his first breakup with Leslie for the millionth time. He suddenly blurted out, "Look, it's just not gonna work out. I don't love you anymore. That's it! It's over!"

Rios had looked over at Noah with a wide-eyed expression that implied he was in the presence of a lunatic and said, "Hey, Gunny, you talkin' to me? 'Cause you're lookin' right at me, and as far as I know, we weren't having a conversation. And also, dude, I gotta tell you; you just broke my heart."

Man, Ricky and I had some good times together, Noah thought. *And we went through some shit together, too. I wonder how he's doing. I've been meaning to call him for months.*

So there it was. The opportunity to shift from thinking about doing the right thing to making it a priority and doing it. When he got back from his run, he ate breakfast and then gave Ricky a call at the last number he had, which was his family home.

A woman who was apparently Ricky's mother answered the phone. She was initially evasive about her son's whereabouts until Noah explained who he was.

"Oh, you're his friend Gunny from the marines! Enrique always talks about you. He said he was going to give you a call because you live in Seattle. Did he ever get hold of you?"

"No, and I was meaning to give him a call, too. How's he doing?"

There was silence on the phone for a few seconds, and then she said in a conspiratorial whisper, "Not very good, I'm afraid. First it started with the nightmares, then he broke up with his girlfriend because she called the cops on him. Then last week he got out of his car and started to beat up the other driver just because the guy honked at him. He's not himself. He says he doesn't want to talk about it, but I know something's wrong."

Noah heard Ricky's voice in the background.

"Who are you talking to Mom? Are you talkin' about me again? Who's that on the phone?"

Noah jumped in. "Mrs. Rios, please put him on. Tell him it's me calling. Tell him Gunny's on the phone."

After some muffled conversation, Ricky finally picked up, but he didn't sound like the old Rios. Noah tried several of their familiar jokes, called him a few profanities, inquired about the health of his genitals. But he couldn't get a laugh out of him. Normally Ricky would have been giving it right back to Noah. Finally Noah got serious.

"Hey, man, you don't sound like yourself."

"No, I'm myself. Who the hell else would I be? But there just isn't much going on. I just got some stuff I'm trying to work out is all."

"Well, to tell you the truth, I've been having a hell of a time figuring out things since I got out, too. Quit my job. Busted up with Leslie. So, I started reaching out to some vets to get some advice and I met some great guys. That's one of the reasons I called. I heard about this group called Team RWB that gets vets together. They're going to have an event in a few weeks in Seattle. I thought maybe we could meet up there."

"Yeah, sure, man. That sounds good." Ricky didn't sound very enthusiastic. There wasn't much to say, and finally the conversation started to peter out. Noah didn't like the way Ricky sounded, and started to grow concerned, so he decided to reach out.

"Okay, then, I'll check out all the details about that RWB event. But, you know what, why don't we grab a beer or something later today?" Noah had a sixth sense that there was some urgency here, and didn't want to let the opportunity pass.

"I'd like to man, but, ya know, I'm sort of busy. But I've got your number, so I'll give you a call if I get some free time." Noah had become an expert at avoiding people who were offering help, so he wasn't about to fall for it.

"Hey, Rios, you know what? I've got a feeling you're bullshitting me. What have you got to do today that's so important?"

"Well, I was gonna look for a job, and I might be meeting up with some friends later, and I had some other things to do."

"Well, I've decided that I'm gonna make you my priority today. So, get your act together, because I'll be coming by to pick you up at exactly 1300 hours." Noah hung up before Ricky had a chance to invent another excuse.

He felt something good stirring inside, but couldn't put his finger on it. Then he figured out what it was. He was locked and loaded and ready for action.

Chapter 7

The Battle Continues

*"The courage of a soldier is heightened
by his need to help his fellow soldiers."*
—J. Bartell

"W hat's your name?" Monica asked as she kneeled down so the soldier could hear her among all the street noise.

"Huh?"

She spoke up and loudly said, "I said, 'What's your name?' My name is Monica, and I served in the 82nd. What branch were you in?"

"I was in the army too. Infantry. My name is Novak. PFC Steve Novak, of the 4th Infantry Division." He gave her a mock salute. She thought he might be high on something.

"When did you process out?"

"That would be in 2011, ma'am. Why are you asking me all these questions?"

"Well, I saw your sign, Steve, and I heard you ask for help, so I want to know how I can help you."

"I'm hungry, lady. If you could give me a few bucks, then I could get some dinner."

Monica handed him a five-dollar bill, and Steve Novak reached for it like he had just won the lottery. He broke into a wide grin revealing several gaps in his front teeth.

"Thanks a bunch, lady." He looked up at her, expecting she would now hurry away, having done her good deed for the day. He could usually count on a few extra-special do-gooders. In fact, every once in a while someone would hand him a twenty. They were usually older men or women who would tell him about the son, daughter, brother, or sister they had lost in Iraq, Afghanistan, or, sometimes, Vietnam. They didn't understand how frustrating it was to listen to them once he had enough money to buy a pint and get some food in his belly. But this one didn't leave. Instead she asked another question.

"How did you wind up here?" she asked, making a gesture that indicated the street and the crush of humanity around them, but really meant his whole general situation.

Steve broke into a laugh that resolved into a look of bitter irony, and his eyes narrowed. "Well, that's a long story, but I don't think it matters that much."

"No, it does matter to me. I really want to know."

"You ever been on the waiting list at the VA?" Monica shook her head. "I didn't think so. You ever get thrown out of the VA?" She shook her head a second time, and was suddenly ashamed of her relative good fortune.

"So, look, thanks for the money, but I'm pretty hungry, so I think I better be going," he said. "But maybe you *could* give me a hand." He gestured toward a wheelchair that was folded in the corner.

Monica reached down and grabbed his arm while Steve raised himself with his cane and leaned against the glass window. It seemed to take all his strength to balance on his one good leg. "If you don't mind, maybe you could open the chair, and make sure you lock the wheels."

When he was settled, she said, "Well, where do you think we should have dinner?"

"Lady—"

"My name's Monica."

"Okay, Monica. You don't really need to have dinner with me. Just help me across the street to that fast-food joint and I'll be able to get myself up the ramp."

Monica didn't know quite how to respond to being so clearly rebuffed, so she just stood in awkward silence behind Steve's wheelchair and waited for the light to change. Her resolve to help started to wane as she suddenly felt conspicuous and a bit ridiculous, and then the stench emanating from her new friend began to overcome her. She was doing her best to fight the wave of nausea she felt descending when the light finally changed and they began to weave through the crowd and across Seventh Avenue.

When they reached the entrance, Steve turned and thanked Monica, but she could see he was embarrassed by the spectacle she had created and the disruption to his routine, however pitiable it was. The man in the wheelchair had a certain dignity and pride, and it struck her how presumptuous it was to attempt to force herself on someone who clearly didn't want her help. In a way, she felt she was being selfish.

"Okay, if you could just open the door, I can make it the rest of the way on my own."

"Are you sure you don't want me to join you for dinner?"

"Look . . . Monica? I know you mean well, but the truth is there really isn't anything you can do for me. I've been in lots of VA hospitals. In the alcohol and drug rehab units, and I always wind up using, and get kicked out. I can't even keep track of how many times at this point, and guess what? I don't really give a damn anymore."

"Well you should care. You can always give it another chance. Maybe this time it'll be different." Monica could tell her words had a hollow ring and sounded naive the instant they came out of her mouth, but, regardless, she was determined to give it her best shot.

Novak let out a mock laugh. "This time it'll be different? Ha. I don't believe that, and my kids don't believe that.

Nobody I know believes that. The last time I called the VA, they put me on hold so long, I finally got disconnected. What's the difference, anyway?"

Monica imagined how her parents would feel if she found herself in Steve's situation. They would scoop her up and bring her home in an instant. He was probably only a few years older than her. "What about your parents? I bet they would like to see you get some help."

"My parents are dead, and they washed their hands of me long before they died. It probably killed them trying to save me. They dragged me off to a bunch of VA hospitals, and I flunked out every time, so they got sick of me, and I can't blame them. So, look. Just let me go have something to eat. I'm starving."

"Are you sure there isn't something I can do for you?"

"You did already. You gave me five bucks, and you helped me get to the door. Thanks a bunch. I'll be fine."

Right at that moment, a tall, skinny man who was apparently the restaurant manager came to the entrance and asked if Steve was bothering Monica.

"No, of course not," Monica said, but she was more embarrassed than Steve was. Steve was used to this sort of treatment, and he and the manager clearly had some history. Then things suddenly got worse.

The manager looked down imperiously at Steve and demanded to see his cash before he would let him through the door, which Steve promptly displayed in ample supply. It was evident he could have afforded dinner even without the money Monica had given him. The manager walked off in a huff, clearly annoyed he couldn't bar Steve from his establishment. Monica finally had to accept that it was time to retreat.

"Well, okay. I guess I'll be going, then," she said.

"Thanks. I appreciate it, I really do. Don't worry about me. I'm fine." Steve was relieved to see her walk away, but she had made an impression on him and planted a seed. For a second, he actually had a little glimmer of hope. Then he wheeled his way through the door and promptly forgot about the incident.

Monica began to weep as she turned and walked away. Her confusion and sense of helplessness were overwhelming.

When she reached her seat on the train, she Googled "homeless vets," and discovered the problem was much bigger than she ever imagined. She found a site called National Coalition for Homeless Veterans that was a wealth of information. It estimated that almost fifty thousand veterans were homeless in America on any given night. But it appeared that help was on the way, because homelessness among vets had declined in the last few years. It also appeared that the VA was working hard to provide permanent shelter for vets. It had finally been recognized that the problems related to PTSD and substance abuse were frequently connected to their service. Vietnam vets had been treated poorly, and the awful truth was that time may have been one of the biggest factors in the recent decline in homelessness among veterans.

That night Monica discussed the events of the day with her mother as they cleared the table after dinner. Her mother sympathized with her daughter's feelings, and assured her she had done her best for the man, and counseled her to try to let it go. Her father happened to walk into the kitchen at that moment and buried his head in the refrigerator, overhearing their conversation. Pretending he was speaking to no one in particular, he said, "I thought no soldier left behind meant *no* soldier left behind." He filched a piece of cherry pie and headed back to the Yankees game, but he had said a mouthful.

*

Noah had never been to Ricky's house, so he didn't know what to expect. From the address he plugged into his GPS, he knew the zip code would bring him to a pretty rough part of town, but he was pleasantly surprised to see that his neighborhood consisted largely of well-kept single-family houses, with kids playing ball along the street, parents pushing strollers, and small but tidy yards in the front of each house.

Ricky was leaning against his fence, wearing a Seahawks jersey with a stogie in his mouth, head ducked down, engrossed in his phone. He didn't notice that Noah had pulled up, so Noah had an opportunity to observe Ricky for a minute while he parked. He definitely looked different than when they had parted company at Lewis almost two years ago. Ricky had gained some weight, grown a bushy beard, and wore a baseball cap sideways. He was making an effort to look "thuggish," which was surprising, because the Ricky Noah had known in the marines always derided that crowd, and was happy to have escaped the influence of some of his high school buddies. Ricky was several years younger than Noah, and Noah's "big brother" instincts didn't like this new picture.

Enrique Rios had been the guy Noah could count on when the going got tough in Afghanistan. Operation Moshtarak, launched in 2010, was, at the time, the largest military operation orchestrated by the coalition forces since the beginning of the war. It had resulted in the retaking of several cities in southern Afghanistan, most importantly the Taliban stronghold of Marjah. The two men had stood side-by-side through some of the fiercest fighting of the war. They had seen and participated in some of the most awful things that could happen in a war zone. As with many soldiers, they had seen things that were never intended for human eyes. They had lived with the constant fear their next step could be their last, should they unknowingly step on an IED. Such things didn't leave one's mind easily. Unfortunately, they also lived with the knowledge that much of their work had been undone in the years since they'd left Afghanistan. Regardless, they'd had each other's backs when it counted.

Despite all they had been through, the Rios who came to Noah's mind was the tall, skinny dude with great speed who had played wide receiver on offense and cornerback on defense in touch football games at their FOB. Ricky would always wear his prized Richard Sherman jersey, sometimes under his PTs. The one he wore today looked more like a maternity top on him. Ricky was letting himself go. Noah knew the feeling.

Noah honked and got Ricky's attention, and his face transformed from a grimace to a wide grin. "Gunny, you freakin' old bastard! How're you doin'?" he shouted.

"Rios! Is that you, dude? With that beard you look like some freaky version of Richard Sherman!"

"Yeah, but I'm as handsome as ever, and you're still as ugly as you ever were."

They went on like that for a few minutes, smoked some cigarettes, and then hopped in Noah's car and headed to a local pub for burgers and a few beers. The beers turned into more than a few and, after catching up on this and that, Noah got around to the subject that was on his mind.

"You know, Ricky, this is harder than I thought it would be." He figured it was time to open up. "I mean, I can't seem to stay on track. Not with my relationships, my career, my health. It seems like every time I start to make some progress, I just give up. And, I've acted like an asshole a few times."

"What do you mean?" Ricky asked.

"Well, you know how much I missed Leslie?"

"Oh, man, tell me. I got so sick of hearing about that broad. Then she went off and got married, and you really went off the deep end. Now she's got a kid, right?"

"Yeah, but she divorced the asshole she married. And the kid's actually not a bad kid. Our breakup wasn't her fault. It was me, my paranoia. I let her get away, and then I got her back when I got home. Now I just push her away, even though she's the best thing to come along my whole life." Noah was telling the truth about Leslie, but his real agenda was to draw Ricky out.

"What about you, Rios? You got a woman?"

"Yeah, I do, but we got problems. She's on my back too much. You know, always asking me about everything. Trying to get me to talk about shit I don't want to talk about. She's got to learn to leave it alone. Just let it be. Sometimes, I don't want to talk to anyone, you know?"

Noah pictured himself sitting in his apartment, avoiding the phone or any form of human contact. He knew the challenges soldiers faced didn't make sense to those around them, but the problems were there, coming back when you thought they were gone, sitting on you until you felt paralyzed. He was only recently starting to get back to normal. His recovery hadn't started until he was finally ready to accept some help.

"But, Rick, maybe she's trying to help you. Your mom said you had some stuff go on with the cops lately—"

"Yeah, well, my mom ought to keep her mouth shut about that stuff. That's what I mean. Everybody's always up in my business. I know what I'm doing. I don't need anybody getting in my face."

"I know. It looks like that, but you gotta look at the facts, man. If you're fighting with everyone—"

"What would you know? Man, you're always so cool."

"Not so. I've been reaching out for help, and things have gotten better. I knew I had to do something because I felt like shit all the time. I quit my job, and I was about two seconds away from jumping across the table and pounding the hell out of my boss when I quit. I knew if I didn't get out of that place, I was gonna do something bad, real bad. Believe me, I know what it's like to feel like you're losing it."

"I don't think I need to do anything, because, Gunny, to tell you the truth, I don't really care."

"Don't really care about what?"

"About anything, or everything. I lie there awake at night. I can't sleep, and when I do, I see some crap I don't want to see. I know what I did. You did, too; we were there together. That shit ain't goin' away."

"Well, we did what we had to do. I don't feel guilty about that, Ricky," Noah lied.

"I guess I feel like I did what everybody else did, but I know my soul is gonna rot in hell for the shit I did. Kids and women and stuff. You know what I mean."

Noah knew the incident Ricky was referring to. Outside of Marjah. Clearing the highway to the south. All civilians had been told to evacuate. Everyone in the town had been given plenty of warning. As they approached on foot, Noah and Ricky had seen a woman and two little boys hiding in a gully near the side of the road, and then suddenly they burst out and came running toward them. Someone behind him yelled, "Bombers, bombers!" The woman was wailing, her face filled with rage, hate, and vengeance. Except later they realized it hadn't been a look of rage but of utter terror, and that her screaming had been that of a mother begging the two soldiers to spare her children. It had all happened so quickly, in just a few seconds. Regardless of what they did after that, things were never the same. And that was only one of dozens of things they had shared during their time together in Afghanistan.

"Well, I was going to a group at the VA for about a year. And it helped to be around other guys who understood. Are you doing anything like that?"

"I tried that shit, Gayhles. It's not for me. It's just talk, talk, talk. All bullshit. I still go home and want to . . ." He stopped in mid-sentence.

"Want to what?"

"You know what!"

"No, what?"

"Nothin'. Nothin'. I don't want to do anything but get drunk. Which reminds me ..." Ricky jumped up and walked over to the bar to order another round. He was clearly trying to change the subject.

Something in Ricky's eyes told Noah this wasn't just idle chitchat. There was a darkness and sadness and hopelessness that permeated his conversation all afternoon. Noah pushed the envelope a little further when Ricky returned with two more beers.

"So, what happened with this road rage thing?"

"Man, do you know everything about me? What else did my mother tell you?"

"Not much, just that you had some incident on the road."

"Some incident? Some incident?" Ricky stood up and pounded the table so hard the bottles rattled, and every head in the pub turned to stare at them.

"That bastard cut me off and almost caused a pileup. You bet I chased his ass down and dragged him outta his fancy car. He's lucky the cops came or I would've snapped his neck." Ricky whipped his fists around in a tight circle, and curled his lips into a snarl. Just then the bartender stormed over and said, "Hey guys, keep it down, or I'm going to have to ask you to leave."

Noah stood up quickly and positioned himself between the bartender and Ricky. "No problem, buddy, we were just leaving," he said and in the same motion corralled Ricky toward the door. The old line of command must have kicked in because he didn't make a fuss, but instead peacefully headed for the door.

Once inside Noah's car, Ricky was a different person. He had gone from loud and violent to completely silent. No matter what line of conversation Noah tried, Ricky just stared straight ahead. His expression didn't betray any emotion whatsoever. So they drove on in silence.

It was starting to turn dark by the time they pulled up in front of Ricky's house, and so Noah didn't notice Ricky was weeping until he heard him exhale and let out a deep sob.

Noah did the only thing he knew how to do; he ignored it, and pretended it wasn't happening. It went on like that for several minutes, until finally, Ricky said, "Hey, look, I'm sorry. I don't really know what's going on with me. One minute I feel fine, the next I want to kill someone, and then the next I want to drive my car into a building. It's not good."

"Well, you've gotta get some help. See a shrink. Go to the VA. Get some help, man. Maybe get some medication or something. I don't know."

"Yeah, sure, man. I'll do all that soon. Don't worry about me."

"Well, I am worried about you. I was going through the same stuff, and then I started making some calls to some vets. These guys were great. They gave me some really good advice. They got me to get into action. I'm getting involved in stuff. I got off my butt and started running and doing PT again. That alone made me feel a lot better."

"Yeah? That sounds like a plan," Ricky offered. He actually sounded hopeful.

"It's more than a plan, bro. It's what we're doing tomorrow."

"What's that?"

"We're meeting over at the track at the high school in Warrenville tomorrow morning at 0800 hours, and we're gonna start to get you back in shape. You up for that? Actually, I take that question back. That's an order, Rios. PT at 0800."

Ricky was silent for a minute and then replied, "You got it, Gunny." Noah was relieved to see a smile come across his friend's face.

"And another thing, Rios."

"What's that?"

"When you show up tomorrow morning, I want that stupid, freakin' beard shaved off. I want to see you clean shaven, old school, right to the skin. You got it, Rios?"

"You got it, Gunny. 0800?" Ricky climbed out of the car, shaking his head in amazement. "Man, I ain't seen that for a while."

Noah drove off, knowing Ricky was in trouble and that a simple run and some PT weren't going to solve his problem. But he also knew he had taken a step in the right direction. By helping his friend he was also helping himself. There was so much the marines had instilled in him that didn't exist in the civilian world, that only another soldier would understand. Sometimes one had to step up and be the one to make things happen. His conversations with Frank, Dino, and Blayne had lifted him, and now it was his turn to lift Ricky. It was true Noah and Rios had shared some moments each would rather forget, but magical forgetting wasn't going to happen. They had gone through these things together, and they had pulled each other through. And now they had work to do. Now they were on their way to their next mission. Together.

Chapter 8

Teamwork

*There are no secrets to success. It is the
result of preparation, hard work, and
learning from failure.*
—Colin Powell

M onica continued to be plagued by the image of Steve
Novak. But life has a way of moving on, and in the
months following, she was soon overwhelmed by
her responsibilities with Justin, dealing with her parents'
health concerns, and balancing her checkbook—all along
with her determination to continue networking so she could
find a new career direction. Then there was the issue of
Peter Macpherson. Monica had followed Tracey's advice
and gone out to dinner with Pete the next time he had asked,
and, as time went on, she had begun to develop strong
feelings for him. He was the sort of man who was both
strong and sensitive, and was a true soldier in that he
presumed if there was a problem, then there had to be a
solution, regardless of how challenging the problem might
be.

For instance, when she told Pete about her encounter
with Steve Novak and her concern, not just for him, but for
all soldiers in a similar situation, she was delighted to learn
that Pete was deeply involved with the issue. He understood
her feelings, and was seeking some practical solutions. He
was spending a good deal of time as a volunteer at the VA
in Lyons, New Jersey, and was considering developing a
career in the field of veteran services.

He explained that substance abuse among vets was a
serious problem, and the challenge the VA faced was

getting people into its programs. Generally those who found success were those who wanted it, but frequently those who most needed help didn't want it, or perhaps weren't yet ready to accept it. Forcing them into a program could do more harm than good by affecting those who were working hard to stay clean and sober. The issue was compounded by the fact that many veterans suffered from co-occurring disorders. So, misdiagnoses were a common occurrence, which only added to the confusion. And then there was the maze of paperwork these veterans were unable to tackle. Additionally, many of these vets had been rejected by their families.

"I know how it feels, Monica. It breaks your heart to see a soldier like Novak destroying his life, and it's frustrating that he won't make the effort. But this is really complicated stuff," Mac explained. "It's the old military story. A catch-22."

"Well, it seems like a catch-22 on steroids, Mac."

"That's true, but it still comes down to trying to help one soldier at a time, which is why I want to be involved in some way." Monica decided that she would also volunteer her time with Pete.

Little by little, Monica was starting to accept that she and Pete were becoming "a couple." He had the good sense to respect Monica's reticence, and his patience was starting to pay off. Without saying anything overt, Pete made it clear he was willing to wait for Monica to come around, and that made her feel truly loved and respected. He and Justin genuinely seemed to like each other as well. However, Monica had yet to invite Pete over to Sunday dinner, partially because she wasn't sure he was quite ready for the full Brady treatment, or perhaps because she saw it as too large a step. Her mother, of course, extended the invitation anytime Pete stopped over to take Monica out.

"When are we going to have you over for dinner, Pete?" Monica's mother would say as they climbed into his car.

"Anytime Monica invites me, Mrs. Brady," Pete would cheerfully reply. It was starting to be a routine, with the two of them pretending Monica wasn't present.

*

One night, over dinner, Monica wanted to learn more about volunteer work regarding veterans. "What do you think you can do to help vets, Pete?"

"I'm not entirely sure what I'll do eventually, but I do see a real need and, well, also a market opportunity. So it's possible I might find a way to mix the two." Pete was working at a hospital in Morristown, but had yet to settle on a career path. He had entrepreneurial aspirations, and wasn't entirely happy working for an enormous medical center.

"Well, I've started to network a bit with veterans. I was lucky enough to meet a really interesting entrepreneur thanks to Tracey Jones, and that has gotten me thinking about starting a business, but I'm not sure what I would do," Monica replied.

"Have you ever thought about franchising? The reason I ask is because I know someone, a woman who knows all about that. She's a vet. Used to be a marine."

"I've actually been thinking a lot about franchising. But it's confusing, and I don't know where I would get the funds to start, so I'd like to learn more about it. Do you think she'd take a call from me?"

"I'm sure she would. I can give her a call to set it up. I met her at an event right before I processed out. She was speaking to a bunch of us, and gave us her contact information. I spent a few minutes with her and she was very generous with her time, and invited me to call her if I wanted to learn more about franchising." Mac scrolled through his contacts and finally came to the name he was trying to find. "Her name is Mary Kennedy Thompson, and she's a top executive with a company that owns a bunch of franchises. I'll shoot the two of you an e-mail and set it up."

Monica exchanged a few e-mails with Mary and finally the day arrived when she was due to call her. She was a little astounded that a person of Mary's stature would be willing to take a call from her. Mary Kennedy Thompson was the COO of the Dwyer Group, a holding company that controlled numerous franchises. Additionally, she was the director of veteran affairs for the company and had been involved with an organization called VetFran. Mary had been a member of the US Marine Corps and risen to the rank of captain. Monica could hardly believe her good fortune, but she was learning that her military affiliation could open many doors.

Monica was surprised that Mary picked up her phone on the first ring.

"Hello, Mary Kennedy Thompson here. Is this Monica Brady?"

"Yes, it is. Thanks so much for taking my call, Ms. Ken—"

"Monica, we're not at all formal around here. My name is Mary, and I'm delighted to speak with a fellow officer. I gather you were with the medevac unit of the 82nd?"

"Yes, I was, and saw action in Afghanistan."

"Well, I was with the marines, and I have to admit I was always in awe of the men and women who were willing to take on that job. My goodness, to put yourself in harm's way to save another soldier really speaks to the heart of what it means to be of service."

"Thanks, Mary. It was a time of my life I'll never forget, and I miss it. And I miss the friendships I developed. It's nice to speak with someone who understands. I know you're busy, so I won't take up too much of your time."

"Don't worry. I've set the time aside. How can I help you?"

"Well, I'm sort of at sixes and sevens trying to figure out what direction to go with my career. I've thought about franchising, but it seems confusing and a little scary. So, I thought perhaps you could tell me a bit about that, and your background, because you clearly seem to have things figured out. I even read online that you're a licensed plumber!"

Mary laughed out loud and said, "Well, I'm not so sure you would say I have things figured out if you could have seen the chaos around the breakfast table this morning, but I try my best to make things work. And I am a licensed plumber. I can tell you there are times in that business when all you're dealing with is chaos, and you'd better be ready to get your hands dirty if you want to fix matters." This comment immediately put Monica at ease. *I may be a janitor now,* she thought, *but I'm speaking with a successful woman who used to be a plumber! Who knows where I might be one day?*

"So, Mary, could you tell me about your background? When did you join the marines?"

"Certainly. I joined the Marine Corps in 1985 when I graduated from the University of Texas. I was commissioned a 2nd lieutenant and, after going through the basics school, became a logistics officer. I was an 0402, which is a logistics officer, military occupational skill."

"I'm just curious. Why did you choose to join the Marine Corps?"

"Because I think they're the best of the best. Actually, I'm an army brat and I grew up in the military my entire childhood, all the way through high school. We traveled and moved and saw a lot of the world, and I knew I wanted to be in the military. As I got more and more involved in the ROTC program, I kept seeing this great group of marines who were dedicated, smart, and all in, and I wanted to be part of that. I actually switched from the army ROTC program to the Marine Corps, got a special scholarship, and never went back. I loved every minute of it."

"I was tempted by the marines, too, but my dad was army, so it just seemed like a good fit. How many years did you serve as an active duty marine?"

"I was in the Marine Corps for eight years—a few years what they call IRR, or the Individual Ready Reserve. I didn't do anything in the IRR. In the Marine Corps I was stationed in Camp Lejeune and then Okinawa, Japan, and then Treasure Island out in California, in recruiting."

"So, how did you go from being enlisted in the Marine Corps to being the COO of an extremely successful company? My biggest question is how I can put my knowledge and experience to use. I've read a bit about franchising, and it seems interesting. How did your military training translate into what you're doing today?"

"I get asked that all the time. I like to speak with veterans who want to get into small business ownership because I think veterans and franchising are a great fit. Veterans understand discipline, they've been taught quite a bit about leadership, and they know systems. Franchising is all about following the system, having the discipline to get it done, and then leading a group of people toward a common mission. It's a good match, and it was for me in particular. I knew I wanted to be in my own business but I had no idea how to do it."

"So how did you get started with franchising, Mary?"

"My husband came home one night from a chamber mixer when we lived in San Antonio and he had a little booklet. It was on a company called Cookies by Design; back then they were called Cookie Bouquet. I kept looking at it saying, 'I could do this.' At the time I was a sales rep. I was rookie of the year and making lots of money, but I wasn't fulfilled. I really wanted to lead a team toward a common mission, a common goal. I looked at this and said, 'I would love to do this, but I don't know how.' Then I turned to the back page and found three magic words: 'For franchising information.'

"For me, those magic words meant opportunity. We say in franchising that you're in business *for* yourself but not *by* yourself. I had no idea what I was doing. I'm convinced I would not have been nearly as successful as a business owner if I hadn't been a franchisee, because the franchise taught me so much. They taught me how to make the product, how to sell and market the product, how to understand my financials. They turned me into the businessperson I needed to be in order to be successful."

"I can't believe you started with a cookie company, and now you're COO of a company that manages and runs several different franchise companies," Monica said. "So you said a lot of your successful franchisees are veterans. Why do you think that is?"

"Well, Monica, I think there are a number of reasons. One is because they get systems. They understand about working within a system and having that discipline. They want to belong to something but they also want to serve. One of the things that has always amazed me about veterans is, when you get to the core of who they are, they have a heart for service. They want to serve their country. They want to serve their duty. With franchising, they can serve their team and their customers while working within a system. It makes sense to veterans.

"It's probably a mindset thing. Veterans get that systems work for a reason, and are less likely to say 'let's reinvent the wheel.' Instead, they'll say, 'Let's follow the system because the system is what's going to get us there.' In all of our eleven brands, the franchisees who most closely follow the system are the most successful. Veterans are more predisposed to that. They understand leadership, whether they were a squad leader, a platoon commander, a battalion commander, in charge of an airplane, in charge of a team that took care of an airplane, or any of those positions. They usually had some significant responsibility and they understand what that means. They have the discipline to pay attention to the details."

"I know what you mean, Mary. When we left on a dustoff, we had to follow protocol, and we had to do it fast. To somebody not in the military, the details might have seemed like a waste of time, but we were basically a lot of young men and women in charge of tens of millions of dollars of equipment and dozens of people. I've seen that executing a plan can make all the difference and that my military experience has given me an incredible background in responsibility."

"Absolutely. My friend Greg Tanner always says, 'I like hiring veterans because they understand commitment. They're the few people who can put on a résumé: "willing to take a bullet for my former employer."' When veterans sign that agreement, they understand, 'These are the requirements. This is what I must do.' And they live up to it. It makes them strong business leaders; it makes them strong franchisees. Because they understand leadership, recruiting the right people makes sense. They get that, and taking good care of the people they hire.

"I teach a class on the eleven Marine Corps leadership principles. I put them in civilian terms. When I share them, people say, 'That's the most brilliant thing I ever heard.' And I say, 'Those are the Marine Corps leadership principles. I didn't invent them. They are what every private, captain, general, and first sergeant in the Marine Corps is taught about how to lead.' They cross businesses, organizations, cultures, and genders. They're remarkable."

"Speaking of gender, Mary, there aren't that many women in the marines. It couldn't have been easy to reach the position of captain, and, of course, you had a lot of men reporting to you. That must have helped you in your career. I found that with the chain of command in place, it really wasn't an issue with men."

"Yes, it's interesting. For me, when I came over to the Dwyer Group to be president of Mr. Rooter, it was like coming home—for two reasons. First, I had grown up in the Marine Corps. I hesitate to call it a "boys' club," but it's a male-dominated field. I always appreciated and understood it. I enjoy working with both men and women. I love following my heart, rather than fitting into somebody's idea of what I should do. I loved serving in the Marine Corps. I jumped out of airplanes, rappelled out of helicopters, and went to foreign countries and did fascinating things. The challenge of it was absolutely thrilling to me.

"Second, the Marine Corps has this code of values. Marines live with integrity. They mean what they say and they say what they mean. The Dwyer Group has a great set of values. We call it living RICH with respect, integrity, customer focus, and having fun in the process. We talk about our code of values all the time. We might have a meeting that's particularly tough and we'll start with a statement like, 'One of our values is communicating with honesty and purpose. You know what? Let's focus on that in our meeting today.'"

"So I looked on your website and it seems like your company is in all sorts of different businesses. Isn't that unusual? I just presumed that a company might be in a market segment, like food or car repair or something like that, but you guys seem to be growing in different categories."

"Well, that's true, and part of what makes us different. We have eleven different brands, but they're all things you would expect to need to take care of your home. Everything from Mr. Rooter for plumbing, to Air Serv for heating and air-conditioning, to Rainbow International for restoration and carpet cleaning, to Glass Doctor for all types of windows and auto glass, to Molly Maid to clean your home, to Mr. Handyman to fix things up, to Ground Guys for your grounds maintenance, to Mr. Electric to fix your electrical, to Mr. Appliance to fix your appliances. We also have Five Star Painting and Protect Painting, as well, to round out our eleven. Those are typically male-dominated trades. As I said, to me, it felt like coming home. When I first stepped in as president and started meeting franchisees, as soon as I said, 'I was a marine,' they gave me grace. They gave me a chance to come in and learn and grow with the brand."

"Do you mind if we talk a few minutes longer? I know you must be busy."

"Not at all, Monica. So tell me, what are you doing now?"

Monica could feel herself hesitate. Then she remembered her talks with Tracey. "So, the truth is I'm not doing what I want to be doing; I'm doing what I have to do at the moment. I lost my husband, who was also in the military, three years ago, and I have a little boy I'm raising on my own. So, right now, I'm working as a janitor."

"That's very admirable, Monica. I can see you are doing what you have to do. There's no shame in that."

"Thanks for saying that, Mary. Coming from someone like you, it means a lot. I really do think of myself as an entrepreneur. The idea of a franchise is appealing because of the advantage of running your own business with some structure and guidance."

"That's exactly it, Monica. I started out as a franchisee at Cookies by Design. I was a franchisee for a number of years. I eventually became a multi-unit franchisee. When I sold them, the franchisor called me and said, 'Would you come work for us?' I joked and said, 'I don't know if I want to go to the dark side.' They said, 'No, really. You can name your title. We just want you to come on board.' My first year I did 130 site visits and built their field program. I did pretty much every job at that company until I was president."

"But that was a different company, not Dwyer?"

"Yep. I kept running into this company called the Dwyer Group and a fellow named Mike Bidwell, who's our CEO, through the International Franchise Association. Every time I met Dwyer Group people, they were remarkable. It reminded me of how I felt when I met marines. Mike said, 'We have this company and we've been looking for a president for some time. We think you're the right fit.' I remember saying to him, 'I don't know anything about plumbing. I can barely spell it. I know cookies and I know gift-giving and I'm already president of a company. I don't understand why you would be interested in me.'

"He said something I've always held close. He said, 'Business is business is business. Good business is about taking great care of your customers, great care of your people, understanding how to market smartly, spending less than you make, and growing your business. That's what good business is. It's not particular to gift-giving or plumbing or anything else.' After some long conversations, I decided to come over as president of Mr. Rooter and I didn't know the first thing about plumbing. I knew how to run and grow businesses, and I knew franchising, but I didn't know plumbing. I made a promise to myself to earn my plumbing license, because one of the Marine Corps leadership principles is to be technically and tactically sound, and I knew it would demonstrate to my franchisees that I was committed."

"I like the idea that 'business is business is business.' It makes a lot of sense, and encourages keeping an open mind. You must have been very dedicated to take the time to earn a plumbing license."

"It took me a long time. It's a four-year process. You have to have training in a lot of different things. It's a hard, hard test. I was surprised at how difficult it was. It gave me a newfound respect for my technicians who had earned plumbing licenses."

"Does someone have to get that sort of training to own a franchise?"

"No, it depends on the business you are going into. You sound like you are right where you are supposed to be—asking all the right questions and networking. I have this franchisee out in Pittsburgh who happens to be legally blind. He's a pretty amazing guy. He would call me at night or text me with study questions. Really technical stuff. He helped me study."

"So what sort of advice would you give me?"

"A couple of things. If you're considering small business ownership, and I have to admit I'm biased, I think franchising is the great American dream. It's provided me with great satisfaction and great wealth for my family. I worked hard for it, but I couldn't have done it without the help of franchising. As a veteran, you're a good fit for it. If you know how to work within a system and have been successful at it, then you have the discipline and leadership training that gives you the foundation to be quite successful."

"So what do you think I should do next?"

"If you're considering franchising, the first place you should go is VetFran.com. VetFran is a group of more than six hundred franchise owners. We give our veterans discounts coming in, and try to match them with other veterans in our system. I sit on the VetFran committee, which consists mainly of veterans in franchising. All we want to do is give back. That is our sole purpose, to give back to our veterans who have served our country. We want to give them the power to prosper, because they've earned it. If they want to do it, we want to give them every opportunity possible."

"What if you just don't know which business area to go into, and don't have the funds to get started?" Monica's present paycheck barely kept her afloat, and she didn't know how she could make ends meet if her parents weren't willing to put her up.

"Working in a franchise is a good way to get started. If you're getting out of the service and you don't yet have the funds to start your own business, investigate the various franchises and find a job at one. Also, some franchisors have great programs that offer discounts to employees of franchisees. For instance, at the Dwyer Group, we have the H.I.R.E program. For every year that an employee of one of our franchisees works at that company, she gets a certain percentage off of her franchise fee."

Monica was writing as fast as she could. She was getting excited about entrepreneurship. But she was starting to feel guilty about taking up so much of Mary's time. However, Mary reassured her she had cleared her schedule for just this purpose.

"Monica, I don't mean to sound sappy, but it's one thing when people say, 'Thank you for your service,' and another when they actually take the time to try to help a veteran. Obviously I love the subject of franchising, so I don't mind talking about it. There are just a few more things you need to know.

"Whatever business you choose, learn that business. Learn it from the ground up. Make the personal commitment to find the funds to go into the business you decide on. But remember, if you wait until you have a great comfort level with the investment, it's like waiting for the perfect moment to have a child. You'll never do it." Monica knew how true that was, and how grateful she was for Justin.

"When you get 80 percent there, if you're willing to step up and take that risk, you can reap great rewards. It's like my dad always told me, 'Luck is when opportunity meets preparation.' So prepare, prepare, prepare. Learn and study. Talk to other veterans who have gone over to the other side. Then, when that opportunity arrives, you'll be ready for that luck."

Monica's heart was thumping.

"Remember what you've done. You've had great responsibility. You've learned more than you think; you just need to learn how to translate it."

"Well, Mary, that sounds very encouraging."

"I don't want to kid you, Monica. Like anything else, this is hard work, and you have to do your homework. Educate yourself. Go to networking events, and take your time to find the right cultural mix for you. It's more important to find a company that fits with your values than to find a concept that personally fascinates you."

"Whew, Mary. You've been great. Is there anything else I need to know?"

"A few things, and then I do have to go. You need to make sure that the company is solid and doing the right things. That's where the franchise disclosure document comes in. Make sure you read it, you understand it, and know what you're getting into. And the last piece of advice I would give you is to pick something you can be passionate about. You don't have to be fascinated with the subject. Passion is about serving—serving a team and leading people toward a common mission."

Monica's head was reeling from all the information she had tried to absorb in the last hour. As she and Mary were saying good-bye, Monica realized she now had a direction. She did have the heart of an entrepreneur, and now she was going to find the courage to take the next step.

Chapter 9

A Morning in October

*"Real integrity is doing the right thing,
knowing that nobody's going to know whether you did it or not."*
—Oprah Winfrey

An October frost was in the morning air as Noah climbed into his car to meet up with Ricky for their prearranged PT session. Because Noah feared Ricky might not show, he sent him a confirming text before turning on the ignition; within a matter of seconds, a text bounced back from Ricky saying he was heading out the door. Noah was encouraged, and felt he'd done the right thing by putting some pressure on Ricky. Noah's trip would take around forty-five minutes, so he was pleased to discover a talk show on the radio that grabbed his interest. The announcer said his guest was someone named Kelly Perdew, a former winner of *The Apprentice*, and author of a book about the leadership principles he had learned as a US Army intelligence officer, which he had applied to his life and career.

Noah turned up the volume, took a sip of coffee, and settled in to listen to the show. He expected it to be a nice diversion during an otherwise monotonous drive—but he was about to hear something that would transform his life.

The show's host, Brian Franklin, spoke in the calm, reassuring tones of a typical National Public Radio announcer as he recited the official bio of his guest:

"Kelly Perdew is the CEO of Fastpoint Games. Fastpoint Games is a leading developer of live, data-drive games that enable clients to engage, reward, and monetize their users.

"Kelly was previously the president of ProElite.com, an online social network that provides tools for combat sports enthusiasts. While Kelly was there, ProElite, Inc., raised over $40 million, inked a three-year exclusive deal with Showtime to air its mixed martial arts fights, and televised the first network primetime MMA fight on CBS.

"Kelly has held numerous leadership positions in such companies as CoreObjects Software, MotorPride.com, K12 Productions, and eteamz.com. Kelly was president of the largest amateur sport portal on the web—eteamz.com—and helped build the company, which is now serving more than 3.2 million amateur sports teams as part of Active Networks. Kelly was a manager at Deloitte Consulting in the Braxton Strategy Practice and served in the US Army as a military intelligence officer and airborne ranger.

"After winning the second season of NBC's hit show *The Apprentice*, Kelly spent 2005 as an executive vice president in the Trump Organization. Kelly earned a BS from the US Military Academy at West Point, a JD from the UCLA School of Law, and an MBA from the UCLA Anderson School of Management. He is the author of *Take Command: 10 Leadership Principles I Learned in the Military and Put to Work for Donald Trump.*

"Kelly is a nationally recognized speaker on leadership, technology, career development, and entrepreneurship."

Brian Franklin chuckled and said to his guest, "So, Kelly, of course I have to ask you what it was like to work for Donald Trump."

"It was an absolutely incredible experience, Brian. The man taught me so much about management, and how to select the right deal to put my energy into, and then how to execute it. We learn in the military about a concept called Commander's Intent, which means that good commanders communicate their goals top to bottom, so that everyone develops the discipline to work toward that goal. Donald has that ability in spades."

"And he is quite a showman as well!"

"That's for sure. There's never a dull moment around him! He is passionate about everything he does."

"Well, Kelly, I know that as a West Point graduate, and then a ranger, you were able to take those lessons and achieve great entrepreneurial success, and you feel an obligation to give something back to our soldiers who are returning to civilian life."

"Yes, absolutely. It's particularly crucial at this time, with so many men and women processing out of the military. The transition can be pretty bumpy, particularly if they aren't prepared."

Noah was just turning onto the highway. He thought, *Man, there aren't any coincidences. Is this guy talking to me, or what?*

"So, in your book, *Take Command*, you distill the ten leadership principles that you feel everyone can apply, not just in their work, but in all areas of life to achieve success. Can you tell us what they are?"

"Sure, Brian, I appreciate the opportunity to share this information, especially with listeners who are ex-military or transitioning out in the near future. The point I want to stress to that group is that all of these principles have already been instilled in you, but it's easy to lose sight of that when you get out of the military, because it's a very confusing time."

"That's a really important point, Kelly. For those of us who never participated in the military, it's hard to appreciate how difficult the transition can be, but we know from the statistics that the incidence of suicide and other serious problems is much greater in that population."

"And that's why there is great urgency to get this message out," Kelly responded.

Noah thought of Ricky and said to the radio, "You got that right, man!"

"So, I'd like to identify the ten principles, and perhaps we can then discuss them. Is that okay with you, Brian?"

"Sure, go right ahead."

"Okay, here goes:

1. Duty. Do what you're supposed to do, when you're supposed to do it.

2. Impeccability. If it's worth doing, it's worth doing right.

3. Passion. Be passionate about what you do, and do what you're passionate about.

4. Perseverance. It's not the size of the dog in the fight, it's the size of the fight in the dog.

5. Planning. If you fail to plan, you plan to fail.

6. Teamwork. There is no "I" in T-E-A-M.

7. Loyalty. Remain loyal, up, down, and across your organization.

8. Flexibility. In all aspects of life, the person with the most varied responses wins.

9. Selfless Service. Give back. And finally . . .

10. Integrity. Take the harder right over the easier wrong."

Noah had pulled over to the side of the road to scribble down the ten principles. Partway through he stopped, wrote down the name of the book, and made a mental note to purchase it later that day as he got back on the road. He wanted to pay attention to the conversation on the radio.

"So, Kelly, let's take the first principle. Duty. Most of us get that concept. But what does it mean to you?"

"In the military, that concept is vital. It can make the difference between life and death in certain situations. And it affects all the other principles. It's about accountability. If I hire someone to do a job, I expect them to suit up and show up as planned. It also has a lot to do with the eighth principle, by the way, flexibility."

"How so?"

"In business, as in battle, circumstances change. A project that might have seemed simple can grow complex; a deadline can be moved up. The fact is you can pretty much guarantee things will change. If you have made a commitment, then that means you are all in, and that means you need to be accountable, even when conditions are less than perfect."

"Particularly if you're an entrepreneur, I presume."

"Especially if you're an entrepreneur, and especially at the start-up phase, when you don't yet have the luxury and protection of a mature business. When I was on *The Apprentice,* I had to adapt to a wide variety of changing circumstances, from opening restaurants to remodeling houses to designing dresses! I mean, designing dresses? What did I know about that? Yet it had to be done."

"So, I imagine flexibility is also closely related to perseverance. Is that correct?"

"Yes, well, actually all the principles are related to some degree, but certainly these two principles are connected. In my life, ranger school was a great example of a situation when perseverance was absolutely necessary. It was the most strenuous sixty-seven-day sprint imaginable. It's a physical, mental, and emotional test that gives soldiers the same sort of stress they could experience in battle. So, you learn to stick with it, even when circumstances, situations, whatever, completely change—even if you are exhausted, hungry, soaking wet, and emotionally stretched to the limit.

"If there are any soldiers listening out there, they know what I mean," Kelly added.

"You bet your ass, I do," Noah responded.

He thought of the time his unit had entered what appeared to be a quiet town, two days after the event on the road outside of Marjah. He hadn't slept for forty-eight hours, and his brains were fried. The horrible, shrieking sound of that mother's screams kept playing in his head. Yet that morning, they had to take the town. Turning back wasn't an option. This Kelly Perdew fellow clearly knew what he was talking about.

"And I imagine that being an entrepreneur, you have to bring a great deal of passion to your work?"

"Definitely. Without that, many of the other characteristics will fall by the wayside when the going gets tough. I don't really think about what I do as 'work,' because I love it so much."

"So, Kelly," the interviewer calmly asked, "how would you say the second principle, impeccability, relates to situations in battle?"

"Well, impeccability is about flawlessness. And that means attention to detail, which is critical in war. It means knowing how many rounds each soldier has left for his weapon, how much weight he has in his pack, and the precise distance and location of where he needs to march. If you're a soldier calling in artillery fire, you'd better be providing accurate coordinates. You can't say, 'Oh, I'm sorry, I was off a little.' The consequences of anything less than perfection are often fatal."

"So, I would imagine that's one of the reasons ex-soldiers make good employees."

"Yes, the military mindset can be valuable. Our young men and women have had to assume an incredible amount of responsibility at a very young age, and employers should take that into account when they are considering veterans for jobs that require these traits."

"So, you cite flexibility as one of the principles, but also include planning. Aren't they at odds with each other?"

"No, not at all. They actually work hand-in-hand. In any endeavor, you must first determine your goal—the long-term goal and the intermediary goals. The long-term goal might remain the same, but the shorter-term goals will change as circumstances change. The key is to focus on the things that matter most to you. Write them down and remember them. List the steps, prioritize them, and then you can really make progress."

This concept hit Noah like a ton of bricks. Consistency was a big missing element in his life. He had been dancing around his goals. He had a vague idea, but it hadn't dawned on him to get specific and write them down. This guy on the radio had hit the nail on the head. *If you fail to plan, you plan to fail.* Noah thought he should write that down and tape it to his mirror, so he could look at it first thing every morning.

"So, Kelly, what's an example of the sort of planning you did when you were in the military?"

"When I was an assistant S-2, I did a lot of preparation of what are called 'battle books.' Whenever our brigade was deployed to any of the world's 'hot spots,' we needed a comprehensive understanding of the terrain, the culture, alternate routes, and things such as the current political situation. We needed to anticipate every need for our troops so we wouldn't have any surprises. Selecting the correct uniforms, shelter, and medicines was crucial. We needed to monitor the weather and even the condition of the roads. Essentially our goal was to leave nothing to chance, but even so (and let me put it this way because we're on the radio), we know that 'things' happen, and so one needs to be flexible and figure out the best workaround in the moment. And that comes around to another principle, which is teamwork."

"Even in the relatively calm environs of a radio station, I can tell you that teamwork is invaluable," Franklin offered.

"Sure, it's necessary in any organization, but unfortunately, in some corporate cultures, teamwork is given a lot of lip service, but not really enacted, and it often shows in the results.

"Every person at ranger school had a 'buddy.' We were paired up on the firing range, the mess hall—you name it. We were never apart. We watched each other's backs. If you were a loner, you weren't going to make it through ranger school. But in the business world, companies hurt themselves by allowing individual silos to develop, and their main priority becomes protecting their own turf. 'My department versus your department' sort of stuff. In the military, in battle, you learn very quickly that your survival depends on the buddy system."

This comment reminded Noah of when they would prepare to go out on patrol. Noah, Rios, and the other guys would all nervously say some version of "Don't worry, I've got your back, bro." They all knew they were heading out to face the unknown, and it wasn't a benign unknown. Some of them might not return. The enemy was out there. It was amazing how cultural barriers and petty squabbles would melt away at those times. *We were all on the same team,* Noah thought. *And all proud to be on the American team. We might have had our differences at times, but, in a war zone, you had better be able to trust the other guys.*

"So, Kelly, let's talk about the three remaining principles: loyalty, selfless service, and integrity. All three of those characteristics seem to be sorely lacking in the business world today—not just on the part of employees, but also on the part of employers. Do such principles still apply in today's world?"

"There's always been a struggle between management and employees to some degree, but I think that in these challenging times, with technology disrupting the status quo so much, it's all the more reason for employers to aspire to these principles. They help keep the company pointed in the right direction. This is another reason why employers should seek to hire veterans, because many of them will bring these traits into the workplace and influence others.

"My dislike of office politics is one reason I became an entrepreneur. I wanted to start a company that wouldn't be mired in office politics. I wanted a work environment that was merit-driven, where everybody had the same opportunities to perform and be rewarded. I wanted to take the best of army training and meld it with what I considered to be the best business practices."

"What about selfless service?"

"You always get back much more than you give, but you have to make the effort. It's most rewarding when you provide service, and keep your good deeds to yourself. There's an old saying, 'Do good and disappear,' and that's a good rule to follow. I suggest people follow the voice inside them that's encouraging them to do service for others. Get involved, volunteer, become a mentor—get out there and help somebody else."

Noah felt pretty good about the fact he was on his way to do just that, and Kelly Perdew was right—you get back more than you give. He felt energized, just by making the effort to reach out to Ricky, though he had no idea how it would turn out.

Brian Franklin was starting to wrap up the interview, and said, "So in preparation for our discussion this morning, Kelly, I looked up the West Point honor code, which reads: 'a cadet will not lie, cheat, or steal, or tolerate those who do.' That seems like an exceptionally high standard, and almost impossible to live up to, wouldn't you say?"

"It certainly is, but think about the positive ramifications of such a code in a society like ours, where so many people turn a blind eye to all kinds of misbehavior. Think of all the times CEOs of public companies don't accept responsibility for what's going on in their companies, with sometimes disastrous results. The fallout is so much worse than if the company had attempted to follow something like the West Point honor code and build it into their culture. Imagine how the bottom line of those companies would improve.

"Not only that, in the case of some products, lives would have been saved," Brian Franklin added.

"That's true, Brian."

"Well, unfortunately, we're out of time, but I'd like to express my thanks to Kelly Perdew, for sharing his thoughts with us today. It certainly has been enlightening."

"It was my pleasure, Brian. Thank you."

The show was concluding just as Noah turned onto the road that led to the field at Warrenville High, and he could see Ricky in the distance. He was decked out in his sweats and was stretching next to his blue Honda Civic. Noah was happy to see that his face was free of the bushy beard and that Ricky seemed truly elated to see him.

When Noah jumped out of his car, he discovered Ricky looked like a different person than he had yesterday, and it wasn't just the beard. It was the attitude. The angry, disgruntled civilian who, just the day before, had implied he had nothing to live for had been replaced by a soldier, ready to take the next hill.

Noah thought back to some of the comments he had just heard on the radio, particularly about the rewards of selfless service. He got all the payback he needed when he heard his friend say, "Hey, Gunny, it's a beautiful day, isn't it?"

Chapter 10

Good, Orderly Direction

*"A place for everything
and everything in its place."*
—Benjamin Franklin

Things were starting to get serious between Pete Macpherson and Monica. She had even agreed to go away for the weekend with him to a franchising event that was being held in Atlantic City. After Monica's discussion with Mary Kennedy Thompson, she had spent a great deal of time researching the subject, and, while she found certain aspects appealing, such as the camaraderie and support, she also found the initial fees a little daunting. And some franchises seemed to be very controlling and involved, while others didn't seem involved enough. However, when Monica saw an advertisement for the event, something compelled her to attend, despite how scary she found the prospect of taking such a big risk.

It was obvious there was a wide range in the quality of the franchises, and in their cultural attitudes. While Mary had certainly been enthusiastic about franchises in general, she also had been insistent that Monica take her time, and do her homework, which fit her personality perfectly. She was cautious, but perhaps a little too cautious at times. At least that's what Pete frequently told her about their relationship. Their weekend away was a big step, but everyone in the Brady family (including her father) had encouraged her to take the trip. Harold had come around after Pete joined the family at a church service one Sunday, and was invited to stay for dinner, which would take place after the conclusion of the Giants game, of course. It was to become a memorable day in their family history.

Pete wasn't a baseball fan, and didn't care one way or the other about the Yankees, but he was a football fan. A serious football fan. Having grown up in the Pittsburgh area, he was naturally a diehard Steelers supporter. Harold and Monica's brother, Elston, were willing to overlook this flaw in his character, because they were delighted to see Monica smiling and cheerful again for the first time in a long time. Harold took his usual seat in his recliner, and invited Mac to sit on the couch next to him, so he could get to know him a little better. The Giants were playing the Eagles that particular Sunday, so they could all comfortably root for the Giants. It was a sort of "the enemy of my enemy is my friend" type of situation. Monica plopped down next to Mac in order to keep an eye on things. Her father sometimes forgot his little girl was already in her thirties, had been to war, and was capable of taking care of herself. She didn't intend to allow her dad to interrogate Mac.

"So, Pete, I hear you and Monica are thinking about taking a trip down to Atlantic City," Harold said.

"Yes, sir. We're very excited to learn all about franchises," Pete replied.

"I've known people to blow a ton of dough at those casinos down there," Harold snorted. "You have to be careful."

"Dad, we aren't going there to gamble. We're going there to learn about franchises," Monica interjected.

Before Harold could inquire about the sleeping accommodations, Monica's mother appeared with a tray of cheese and crackers, and deftly moved the conversation toward safer turf.

"So, Mac, Monica tells me you two met when she was in Womack down at Bragg after she fractured her ankle. You were stationed there as a nurse. Is that the sort of thing you're doing now?"

"It is, but I'm looking to go into a more specialized field," he replied.

"Oh, and what's that?"

"I have an interest in trying to help vets who suffer from PTSD and other related problems, such as substance abuse. I've seen how that can destroy families, and so I'm going to be taking some courses that focus on that topic." Mac had a personal investment in the subject because he had lived through the devastation of alcoholism and drug addiction in his family as he was growing up. Obviously he didn't want to discuss that, so instead he mentioned Private Novak, the man Monica had unsuccessfully tried to aid in New York City.

"Veterans such as that fellow Monica tried to help in the city are the toughest cases. Once they head down the road of failure, they tend to give up, but they shouldn't."

"Why is that?" Elston asked. "I think the government's just throwing good money after bad trying to help someone who doesn't want help. Especially if they've already given him a chance and he hasn't been able to kick the stuff."

Mac carefully considered his answer. He knew Elston was expressing the conventional thinking. If somebody is a junkie, he has to hit bottom before he's ready to get help, and if he doesn't make it, well, then he's just collateral damage. It's presumed he's to blame for his addiction, and so less deserving of help. "You know, El, the military used to take that view, and to a degree they still do, but things are changing. Now there are some new medications that can be helpful, and the VA also recognizes that frequently our soldiers are suffering from several disorders at the same time. Sometimes it looks like a guy is a hopeless case, but with the right attention, and treatment, he can be saved." He didn't add that there was a strong spiritual component to a person's success, but Pete firmly believed that to be the case.

Monica jumped in and gave Pete a hug. "Well, I think it's admirable that you're trying to do something to help veterans like Novak. We can't forget the service they gave to this country."

Harold had studied Pete's face for a few seconds, and then suddenly reached out and grabbed his hand. "You're doing the right thing, young man." As luck would have it, at the very instant they clasped hands, the Giants scored a touchdown. Thereafter, it became a tradition for Pete and Harold to shake hands at the kickoff of every Giants game, while sitting in exactly the same seats. The only exception was on those occasions when the Giants faced the Steelers.

*

Though it was now November and many of the attractions on the Atlantic City boardwalk were shut down for the season, it was still a hubbub of activity, particularly around the convention center. The exhibition floor was teaming with people. There were several hundred exhibitors with flashy booths, designed to lure anyone who was passing by. The attendees ranged from those who were serious about investing, and ready to make a decision that day, to some who were just curious, to some, like Monica, who were more than curious, but not yet convinced.

It appeared that every conceivable subject area was covered. Food services and fitness seemed to dominate, but there were all types of services, such as housekeeping, elder care, transportation, party planners, real estate franchises, plumbers, electricians, handyman services, accountants, nursing care, dog training, self-publishing, music production—you name it. The floor was loaded with a dizzying array of opportunities. It was all a bit daunting; rather than encouraging Monica, it confused her and gave her a queasy feeling.

She and Pete stopped by a few booths, and chatted with the representatives from various franchises, but generally found the salespeople to be too aggressive. And so they collected brochures destined to wind up in the garbage in the next few hours. Just when they were starting to get discouraged, they noticed a flashing sign at the end of the corridor with a scrolling message saying something about an event specifically for veterans. The seminar was starting in a few minutes, and promised to provide information on loans and other benefits established by certain companies to help veterans get started in franchising. Free doughnuts and coffee were promised, which closed the deal. They headed off to the conference room.

There were several helpful people at the back of the room from banks and a few franchises focusing on vets, as well as the organization Mary had mentioned, VetFran. Mac and Monica gathered brochures and learned about some veteran-friendly franchises, and then found a table when the event organizer announced she was about to introduce the first speaker.

"Good morning. I would like to introduce our first presenter of the morning, Angela Cody-Rouget.

"Angela is a founding partner of Major Mom and one of three certified professional organizers in Arizona. She is also a certified family manager. She moved with her family and the military over twenty-seven times. Because of this, she learned to keep her load light and not get attached to stuff. Angela understands what it's like to make new friends and then have to leave them. Angela Cody spent eighteen years dedicated to serving her country in the US Air Force. She attained the rank of major and resigned her commission to be more available to her husband and two children. She worked as a corporate sales representative for five years and then started her organizing company. She earned a BA in speech communication at Indiana University and an MBA from the University of Colorado. Today, Angela puts a high value on her church, family, friends, and staff, and cherishes those strong connections. She views herself as part of a larger global family, and longs for her business to grow so she can further help those in need—especially children.

"Angela is a member of the National Association of Professional Organizers, also known as NAPO, and Faithful Organizers, and has served as president of the board of directors for NAPO-Colorado. Like most women, she sometimes feels torn between kids and career and the balancing act is difficult, but she's thankful for a husband who is supportive and understanding and she couldn't do life without him. Frederic, who was born and raised in France, is the man with whom she exchanged salutes over twelve years ago. Since Angela is 75 percent German (and everyone knows Germans are known for their strongly regimented lives and organization), it's been an interesting blend of backgrounds! When Angela isn't organizing, you can find her spending time with her children, hiking in the foothills, working on her book, or cooking fabulous meals."

After a few additional formalities, Angela stepped up to the microphone. Monica instantly took a liking to her, even before she said a word. She seemed to be a serious, yet friendly woman, who carried herself with the countenance of an officer. Her dark hair and glistening eyes just added to her appeal, and her enthusiasm for her subject was infectious. She seemed to really care about people, so rather than focusing just on business, her talk was remarkably personal.

"Thank you for that wonderful introduction. Just to give you a little background, I was a major in the air force when I had my first child. My nickname became Major Mom. I would get home from duty in uniform, and my husband would run to the door with baby Lily and say, 'Major Mom is home.' Sometimes men are not great with the little infants and babies; they're so much better with kids when they're older." This brought a chuckle from the women in the audience. It reminded Monica of how fortunate she had been that Danny was willing to sacrifice his military career in order to take care of Justin when she was deployed to Afghanistan.

"My husband was always happy to see me come home. He would hand her to me and say something like, 'Your turn.' This went on until our second child was born, eighteen months later. As a major in the air force, I had two kids under the age of two, and my husband was running his real estate business. At some point we decided that having the nanny, the maids, and the lifestyle I always dreamed of was not the lifestyle we wanted for our kids.

"We wanted the mom—me—to be more available to them and more in tune. Quite frankly, anyone who was in the military gets it. When you're needed to go anywhere at any time, you really do want to go. Even though you love your family, you've been indoctrinated into the military way of life, and you go. Not to say you'd volunteer for dangerous duty, but you're always putting the military first." Monica could appreciate the dilemma Angela was describing, having lived through it herself.

"Your family always comes second. By the nature of the missions you do—I was in nuclear weapons—you have to be that way. At some point I decided that military life and motherhood were incompatible with the kind of mom I wanted to be. It's not wrong for everybody, but I realized that I wanted to raise my kids; I didn't want them to be raised by a nanny.

"So I resigned my commission in the air force, got out, and decided to be a stay-at-home mom for a little while. It was great to take a year off and really bond with the children. I was doing some real estate on the side and some fun things to earn income in the family business. Then the family business tanked and that's when the bottom dropped out of our whole world. We had, well, I should say I had no entrepreneurial skills. I had been out of the workplace for a while, and the job market was gone at that point." Pete leaned over to Monica and whispered "She's an incredibly honest person. I don't know that I would have the guts to stand up there and be that upfront."

"So, people often ask me if I ever had an 'a-ha' moment, when it just hit me that I needed to change what I was doing. There are probably many of you sitting in the audience who might be at a similar turning point, so I'll back up a bit and share that story, and then take some questions.

"I think it really hit me one day after I had entered reserve duty. It was post-9/11, and we were working every weekend and during the week. I had a corporate sales job with lots of fringe benefits and wonderful things, but the military needed us more after September 11, due to the large-scale deployments our command post unit was tasked to manage. So, I'd be gone every single weekend, work all week at the corporate job, and then help manage e-mail communications and assemble asset and troop reports for the 10th AF commander. I was completely, as always, dedicated to the military mission. I'm wired that way. I'm very loyal and I couldn't seem to save time for my husband. Obviously I was making time for the kids because I was their mother, but my head wasn't in the game. My head was always asking, 'What's going on in base? What do they need? What do I need to do?'

"One day I was on duty at Peterson Air Force Base in Colorado Springs, Colorado. We were at this really important meeting. We were getting ready to test a bunch of expensive, important software and equipment and I just couldn't concentrate. It's kind of an embarrassing story, but one I think some of the women in the audience will relate to. I was still breastfeeding my daughter, and so I would bring this breast pump to work, in the military. Even if you've never had to do it, you can imagine what kind of jokes come about with that! Of course I would have to leave to go in the bathroom. Never before in my life in the military would I have considered leaving a meeting led by a colonel, but I did. I got up. I went to the bathroom and I pumped and I almost didn't go back to the meeting. Something was happening inside me where I thought, 'I just don't care what he's saying. I'm concerned about my son, my daughter. How are *they* doing? Is the nanny taking good care of them? Is she loving them? Hugging them? Holding them?'

"It happened just like that. That night, I came home and told my husband, 'I've got to resign my commission in the air force. I need to be home with the children. I need to be more available. I'm their mom. I can teach them our value systems. I'm a godly woman and I need them to learn these things from me.' He was completely floored. He said, 'What? What do you mean? You already quit your corporate job. And now the military? This is our steady income right now.

The business is failing; this is paying our bills.' I said, 'I can't. I need to—you need to—figure something out. I need to be with the children.'

"I never saw it coming. Ever since I was eighteen years old, I'd been driven. I was the cadet commander in ROTC. I always pictured my life with nannies and maids and help. I visualized being a general someday; I saw my whole life in the military. Leaving was a shock to me, my husband, and my family. I assure you, anybody who's getting out of the service who's put in as many years as I had . . .well, many people told me how stupid I was being. A few even said, 'You've lost your mind; you're in postpartum depression; don't do it; you're so close to retirement; you've put in thirteen years.' I can't tell you how often I heard it. So many people were mad at me for making what appeared to be such a stupid decision. But it was clear to me I had to put my family first."

And then Angela told the inspirational story of how her company was born. She was on a mission to encourage the other veterans in the room, and continued, "So, here I am: I have a master's degree in business, I was a major in the air force, we had run a successful business, but the market had fallen out of the real estate business in our area at that time. It was a difficult time for us. One day my husband said, 'You're really organized and you love organizing. Maybe you should do what those people on TV do for a living.' I thought, 'That is ridiculous. I'm not going to organize people's houses for a living. I like to do it for fun, for friends and family.' At first, I couldn't see it being a real business, but I ran upstairs and Googled "professional organizer" and found the National Association of Professional Organizers. I joined that day.

"Lo and behold, that was in 2005 when he gave me that idea. Now, in 2015, here we are with sixteen employees and four different locations. Major Mom is raising up an army of organizers to help other people live with less clutter in their lives, have organized homes, and run better households. That's the short version of the story, if you believe that!" Angela laughed at the irony of her story. There was a round of applause from the audience, and then someone stood up to ask the first question.

The question came from a woman who appeared to be in her forties. "Thanks for being so honest about your background. I'm a mother of three teenage children, so we have college sitting in front of us, but I'm here because both my husband and I want to have more fulfilling careers, and want to be more in control of our destiny. We also want a better work-life balance. So, I guess my question is personal, because my husband and I can't quite seem to make that leap. It sounds like your husband was in shock because of the challenges he was going through with his business, and then all of a sudden the income just stopped. What was that like? That had to be scary."

Angela hesitated a moment to think back to that time. "It was awful. I had been one of the two breadwinners in the family from the day we met, until the day I quit my corporate job and my military job. I went from being a breadwinner to not bringing in any income, at the same time our real estate appraisal business was tanking. That decision to get out and be a mom was put to the test over the next . . . let's see, our kids are nine and eleven now, so really, the last ten years. I assure you there were several times when my husband looked at me and said, 'You did not make the right decision. We're short selling our house.' Our house was underwater.

It was worth eighty-five to ninety thousand less than we owed.

"The bottom was dropping out. By that time we had gone through all our savings. We were good savers and had a good credit score. We really were super-responsible Americans. When the bottom drops out and you have no income, you do one of two things." Angela paused for a second before she got to her point.

"You either turn to God and realize who's really in control, or you turn to yourself and you think you're responsible and can fix everything. That's an interesting position to be in when you decide to become an entrepreneur. Most entrepreneurs probably do believe, like I do myself many days, that you are the one who makes it happen; you're in control, and it's all about you. Through the journey of entrepreneurship over the last eight years, I've learned I have very little control over much, except for creating a vision and a mission for the business and, of course, holding myself and everyone accountable in our company."

Pete reached over, took Monica's hand, and squeezed it. Faith was the linchpin of their budding relationship, and here was a real-life example of a husband and wife team who had chosen to live their faith. Monica was in awe of someone who not only had the courage to live her faith, but also to stand in front of a group of people and share her journey, bumps and all.

Angela looked skyward, and then continued, "So much is out of your control. Certainly that's true in the military. We're used to nothing being in our control in the military. That's why I think we make great entrepreneurs. Some general or colonel is always changing the plan, or some other condition changes, and you have no idea why. Other times, something needs to change but never does, and again you have no idea why. People in the military are used to not having control over their lives."

The next question came from a young man, who appeared to be in his early twenties. "I have just processed out, and I'm thinking of going into my own business, or perhaps buying into a franchise. I was going to use my GI Bill to complete my education, but I'm anxious to get started on my career, so I might not. Was your college education helpful in your career?"

"Absolutely it was, and I would advise you to get some type of business training, even if it's an entrepreneurial school with a one-year program. I had to earn a master's degree to make major, so I chose a master's in business and, yes, some of those principles were very helpful in starting the business. There's one thing that is difficult, and I want to make sure I share it with anybody listening who is getting out or contemplating leaving the service. There's something unique about the military. They train you, train you, train you, and train you some more—and then train you some more. Then you finally get to go do what you were trained to do. In the entrepreneurial world, there are some good training programs out there, but nothing like the training we're used to. You complete a couple of programs and afterward you feel like you're flailing out there on your own. There's a good reason why so many veterans are buying businesses and buying into franchises—it's because the systems are already in place. It's something they can follow, and they're good at that.

"Sometimes I think, it was such a long, hard road just getting the business up and running. Keep in mind, I wanted to have a business beyond myself. I wanted employees, I wanted to build a team of organizers, and I wanted to build something that could be sustained past just me. I didn't want to be a solo practitioner. That's an even tougher row to hoe.

"I should add that while formal education is important, you should also educate yourself. The evolution of Major Mom definitely started with one ignorant girl who finally started growing up and becoming an entrepreneur after reading a fabulous book called *Rich Dad, Poor Dad*. I read it while on night shifts as a missileer. *Rich Dad, Poor Dad* really messed with my mind—in a good way. Another book I read that influenced me was *Think and Grow Rich*. I became almost obsessed with reading books about how to create million-dollar businesses. If it's out there, I've read it. So, my advice, young man, is to get a good education, but never stop learning."

Angela looked over at the organizer of the event and announced they had time for one more question. Monica immediately popped up out of her chair and raised her hand. Angela called on her.

"First off, I want to thank you for being so honest about the challenges you faced, and also for speaking up about your faith. I'm a single mother of one child, and after serving with the 82nd in the medevac unit, I left the military about three years ago, because I needed to care for my son. I've sort of dug myself into a financial hole, and, for a variety of reasons, I'm now employed as a janitor, but I'm determined to make a big life change like you did.

"But, I'm in my mid-thirties, and I feel like I'm getting a late start. I was wondering how it was for you, when you made the decision to go into business for yourself. Can you share a little bit about that?"

"Sure. The first three years, I did okay. I had to wait tables and do other jobs to put groceries on the table. I'm not a proud woman; I don't think anything is beneath me.

But there I was, thirty-eight years old and waiting tables! My husband was underemployed as a preschool teacher so our kids could get 50 percent off tuition. It was a really rough time.

"However, once I locked on to the Major Mom vision, I decided that failure was not an option. I was willing to do whatever I needed to do to make it happen. I drew up a financial plan that projected how much money I could expect to be making in years 2006, 2007, 2008, 2009, 2010, and 2011. I asked myself, what do I want this organizing business to be? Just because I was waiting tables at the time didn't mean I was giving up. It just meant I was willing to help support my family.

"I remember when my boss at the restaurant questioned the number of hours I was working. I said, 'I told you when I started that I'm a professional organizer. I'm growing my business and that really is my goal. My goal is not to be here at this restaurant. But when I am here at this restaurant, I'm all here. Whatever I do, I'm going to do it well.'

"Eventually, I started getting so many organizing jobs, I was able to stop being a waitress and go full-time into organizing. If I hadn't laid out a vision of what I wanted, and stuck to my goals, I might never have achieved them.

"I should add one more thing. It's not just about me. Entrepreneurs create jobs. Major Mom creates orderly homes for people. We are creating positive change in the lives of people who need our help. I'm on a mission here, people. It's not just about the money. Money doesn't get you up in the morning, but your mission does. However, it is nice that the money has begun to flow and grow. Thank you."

The audience was moved by Angela's words and rose to give her a standing ovation as she descended the stage.

Monica ran outside the meeting room to catch up with Angela and thank her for her inspiring talk. After a few minutes of exchanging pleasantries, Monica said, "Angela, the last few years have been difficult for me. When I said I was a single mom, that was just part of the truth. My husband died at thirty-eight, very suddenly."

"I'm so sorry to hear that, Monica," Angela replied.

"Thank you, I know you mean that. The point I'm trying to make is that your experience of an 'a-ha' moment, and your determination to carry on despite all of the difficulties, has truly helped me." Monica had something she wanted to say that was embarrassing, but she was determined to say it and hoped Angela would take it the right way. "I felt I needed to come here this weekend. I mean, I felt there was a reason. What I'm saying is, I think coming here to hear you was God-directed."

Angela took both of Monica's hands, smiled, looked her in the eye and said, "Well, I have absolutely no doubt about that, because everything is."

Chapter 11

Start Me Up

*"New beginnings are often
disguised as painful endings."*
—Lao Tzu

A week after Noah and Ricky began meeting up every morning for a run and some PT, Noah awoke to the sound of his alarm and discovered he had a splitting hangover. The night before had begun as a quiet evening. He had been pleased with himself for eating a healthy salad, and limited himself to a single glass of white wine. He had settled in to watch *Sunday Night Football* when he got an unexpected call from an old friend who went by the name of "Trash Head Tom" in high school. Tommy was the sort of fellow Noah's mom would have called a "bad influence," but the truth was that Noah could generally keep up with Tommy, and sometimes outdo him when it came to getting wasted. He probably would have survived the evening pretty much unscathed except for the fact that somewhere along the line, they had run into another old friend, who was carrying some serious weed. Before Noah knew it, it was three in the morning. Or way past his bedtime for an 0700 wake-up call.

He crawled out of bed and peeked out the window, terrified of what he might find. Much to his amazement, he discovered his car was parked in front of his apartment building. "Parked" was a rather generous description for a vehicle that appeared to have been abandoned by the driver after it was slammed against the curb. To make matters worse, the back bumper was jutting into the street by several feet. Noah was amazed there wasn't a parking ticket stuck under the windshield wiper. He had no idea how the car had gotten there. *It must have driven itself,* Noah thought, because he had no recollection of driving home. He was certain of one thing; there was absolutely no way he was going to be able to make his morning meet-up with Ricky. He rummaged around on the floor until he located his pants, searched his pockets, and eventually found his phone and punched in Ricky's name.

"Gunny, what's going on, man?" Ricky was being way too energetic and cheerful for Noah that morning.

"Hey, listen, man. I've got a problem. I tied one on last night . . . I feel like shit. There just ain't no way I'm gonna make it this morning." Noah realized that just the sound of his own voice made his head ache.

"Now wait a minute, dude! You're the guy who got me into this in the first place. It's like the old days. No excuses. Remember? Nada. None. Zero. You made me swear! Get moving. I'll meet you down at the field at the regular time." And then he was gone. Noah stared at his phone and was tempted to throw it across the room. He realized he had created a monster in Ricky. Once that guy got his motor running, there wasn't anything that could stop him.

That's the way it went for the next few weeks. Some days Noah was down and Ricky picked him up and other days Noah needed to get Ricky turned around. It was usually Ricky's anger that caused his problems. His outbursts seemed to come out of nowhere. So, without ever discussing it, they developed a system of supporting each other. Ricky encouraged Noah to apply for college and cut back on his drinking, and Noah talked Ricky out of a tree once or twice every week.

They decided to sign up for a half marathon at a Team RWB event that was going to be held the weekend before Veteran's Day, and followed that night by an event sponsored by American Dream U, where a group of veterans who were successful entrepreneurs would be speaking. They drove up to Gig Harbor early on Saturday morning so they would have time to check into their hotel, pack on some carbs, and get changed well in advance of the start of the marathon.

There were several hundred attendees who had turned out, along with family members, so the place was packed with people and filled with energy. Both Ricky and Noah bathed in the military vibe that was in the air. Just the simple act of signing in and being assigned numbers made them feel as if they had arrived home. There was a certain respect, acceptance, and appreciation of one another as members of a special class who all shared a common experience.

The ex-soldiers ranged in age from their early twenties to their nineties. There were even a few fellows there who had served in World War II. Before they knew it, they had fallen into conversations with men and women who were in fact strangers but instantly felt like old friends. The conversations inevitably hinged on familiar topics such as when and where they had served and in which branch, along with a smattering of personal anecdotes. It wasn't long before Noah and Ricky naturally fell in with a few other marines as they gathered to start the race. By the time they crossed the finish line, they found they had made some new friends. This sort of camaraderie was exactly what they both needed. Noah was grateful he had picked up the phone to speak with Frank those many months ago, who in turn had introduced him to Dino, who had connected him with Blayne, who had introduced him to Team RWB. It certainly beat sinking into the couch with a six-pack and an overflowing ashtray.

That night Noah and Ricky went over to the ballroom where the Veteran Entrepreneurs event was being held, and, as luck would have it, they wound up sitting on either side of one of the after-dinner speakers. His name was Steve Blank. When they went around the table and introduced themselves, they discovered that the army, air force, navy, and marines were all represented. Steve was the last one to introduce himself, and simply said, "Well, I'm air force, Vietnam era, and I've been involved with a bunch of start-ups in technology and other areas, and now I teach at Stanford."

The waiters started pouring some wine, and everyone around the table began to chat with one another, so Noah picked up the program and read Steve Blank's short bio.

> Over the last thirty-five years, Steve has been part of or cofounded eight Silicon Valley start-ups. These have run the gamut from semiconductors to video games to personal computers and supercomputers (MIPS, Zilog, Rocket Science, SuperMac, Convergent Technologies, Ardent, ESL). Steve's last company was E.piphany, an enterprise software company.

> Steve is a former board member of the California League of Conservation Voters (CLCV), Audubon California, Peninsula Open Space Trust (POST), and Startup Weekend. He served as a governor's appointee to the California Coastal Commission.

> Steve currently teaches entrepreneurship at UC Berkeley's Haas School of Business, Columbia University, New York University, Stanford University School of Engineering, and University of California, San

Francisco. In 2009 he was awarded the Stanford University Undergraduate Teaching Award in the Department of Management Science and Engineering. In 2010, he was awarded the Earl F. Cheit Outstanding Teaching Award at the Haas School of Business. In 2011 the National Science Foundation adopted his Lean LaunchPad class as the US standard for commercializing basic and applied research via the Innovation Corps. All his course material is open-sourced at http://steveblank.com/slides/.

His article on the Lean Startup was the cover story of the May 2013 *Harvard Business Review*. It can be downloaded from www.steveblank.com.

Noah could hardly believe the friendly, self-effacing, casual guy sitting next to him was the same Steve Blank he had read about, who was considered to be one of the granddaddies of Silicon Valley.

Steve turned to Noah. "So, Noah, what branch did you say you were in? Marines? Were you deployed?"

"Yeah, I was in the marines, with my buddy Rios, here. We went over to Afghanistan in 2010, during Operation Moshtarak. I got out around two years ago now. And you were in the air force? During Vietnam? What made you decide to join?"

"Yeah, man. That was a different time," Ricky chimed in. They all knew what he meant. These two young men had seen the shocking images from that war, and knew it was a time when returning veterans were not held in the same high regard as they were today.

Steve smiled wistfully and said, "It was during Vietnam. I had dropped out of school and had no idea what I wanted to do. I knew I needed some discipline in my life. The truth was, I had grown up in a pretty chaotic household. I probably instinctually figured out that the military would be good for me, in terms of both discipline and skills. I wish I could tell you I was clear-headed or mature enough to know that for sure. It turned out I was right."

"So, what did your parents think about you dropping out of school and signing up when the Vietnam War was going on?" Ricky asked.

"Well, I didn't tell anybody where I went. I told them the day I was leaving basic training. They all thought I was dead. I was only eighteen, and you do some pretty stupid things when you're that young, huh?"

Noah and Ricky shook their heads knowingly.

"Yeah, I figured if I couldn't make it, I'd just claim I was gay or stupid or something to get out of basic training. I had an experience of basic training right out of movies." Everyone at the table laughed at that, and Steve continued.

"In boot camp, you got the typical drill instructors—even in the air force. We just got into Lackland Air Force Base for basic training. We were on a bus around midnight, heading to our barracks. They told us which squadrons we were attached to. They called out the first squadron and those guys got off the bus. I looked out the window, and there was a drill sergeant, about six feet tall, yelling at them in a way I'd never heard people get yelled at before. Holy cow! We went to the next squadron. More guys got off the bus. This drill sergeant was like two inches bigger, yelling and screaming some more. Third group, the guy was probably six-foot-four. I went, 'Aw, fuck.' It wasn't even day one."

Everyone around the table remembered their own boot camp experiences.

"Finally, we're the last stop. We get off, and I'm looking around, wondering how big this guy was going to be. I still remember, he was like five-two. This little guy named

Sergeant Gonzales. I still remember his name. He was the sweetest guy you could have imagined."

"Way to go, Spanish guy," Ricky said with a smile.

"Yeah. It turned out basic training was hard but fun. Maybe 'fun' is the wrong word, but it wasn't the hell the rest of my guys were going through. It was just the luck of the draw. But luck runs both ways. For instance, when I enlisted, they said, 'Oh, you scored great. You can get into any electronics shop you want.' I said, 'I'd like to learn how to repair computers.' And they said, 'Oh, just tell them that when you get there.' They guaranteed me electronics, but of course the need in the military at the time was electronic warfare, which I had never heard of and never would have picked.

"So it turns out they sent me to electronics school for nine months. It was pretty advanced microwave and electronic equipment. Then I ended up getting assigned to the cushiest base in the states—Homestead right outside of Miami. But my first week on base someone came into the shop asking for volunteers to go to Southeast Asia. Everyone else laughed. But I raised my hand and volunteered for that."

By this point everyone at the table was riveted to Steve's story. A woman who was a navy veteran said something about never knowing what you're getting into when you volunteer, but that joining the navy was the best thing she ever did as well. Then she said, "It sounds like things worked out pretty well for you, Steve."

"Well, you know, showing up is 80 percent of the battle. Life is full of infinite possibilities," he replied. "You just don't know what they are. The first step is just putting yourself in the place where you get access to more possibilities. That's why I volunteer for everything.

"There are some possibilities we obviously know lead to bad paths, drugs and alcohol and addictions and whatever, but with others we don't know where they're going to head. You can choose the path that's wired for certainty, or you can choose the path that's wired for uncertainty, which sometimes leads to adventure. I believe the human race still exists because there's always been some small percentage of the population that wonders what's over the next hill.

"Most humans were probably happy when they found a valley with enough food and said, 'We're hanging here.' But, due to what I'm convinced is some genetic aberration in brain chemistry, others were curious and kept going. Most of those got eaten, but a couple came back and said, 'There's a lot more stuff over here.' I think this genetic aberration has continued. That's why everybody doesn't do what we did, but why there's a small percentage that do."

"So do you think veterans have the curiosity or skills to be successful entrepreneurs?" Noah asked.

"Well, there are a couple of things. There's curiosity, but there's also the ability to operate in chaos. I think the military tends to put young people in those situations, particularly in combat but in other ways as well. It's almost the cruelest training imaginable, but you need that if you wind up in battle. That's what basic training does, because if you can't hack it there, for God's sake, you're not going to hack it when the shit actually hits the fan. That's why Delta Force has its training program. Entrepreneurship is kind of like that.

"Combat is the ultimate test of that.

"You either assimilate data rapidly and make good enough decisions on insufficient data and live, or you make stupid decisions and die.

"Entrepreneurship is not physical life and death, but it's certainly business life and death. So that's the survival part. The curiosity part is, again, always wondering what's over the next hill. As I said, most of the time that can get you killed, but other times it allows you to discover new opportunities others haven't found.

"Curiosity and the ability to be agile and operate under chaos are opposite sides of the coin. You can manage in chaos, but wish you were home, living in comfort, and never want to do this again. Okay, then you'll get a good job, and never think about being an entrepreneur. Or you could realize that you're actually good at it, that it's an employable skill, and combine it with other skills."

Having just applied to return to college, Noah was interested in Steve's unusual educational background. "Steve, I read somewhere that you never finished college, but I also know you worked in the tech industry. I'm going to use the GI Bill to go back to get my degree, because things are different now, but it sounds amazing that you made it without a degree, you know?"

"Yeah, I went back to school and then dropped out again. I managed to get thrown out of some great schools. I just didn't do well at school. I find the educational process is tuned for students who learn in a mainstream way. We now know there are different ways that kids learn. I was somewhat of an outlier. I learn by doing and apprenticeship. Today I happen to teach kids who will learn well in the mainstream environment, which I never could. I find it ironic.

"But some of the best schools I went to weren't Stanford or Berkeley, but military technical training schools. I probably learned more there than anywhere else in my life. They were probably the best vocational schools in the world at the time. I learned how to maintain and operate some of the most complex equipment in the world and I learned pretty well. I was great at it. I love that stuff."

"I heard this guy named Charlie Hoehn speak at an event like this," Noah said. "He said go out and do free work and learn, and then be so valuable that they want to keep you on board. It seems that finding a great mentor and learning like an apprentice is a great way to get ahead."

"I agree with that," Steve replied. "When I was first in the workplace, I kept thinking every day they were going to make me pay to work there. And the truth is I would have done it. If you do what you love, then you stop worrying about instantly maximizing your salary. It's not that you don't negotiate for it, but you're more interested in maximizing how much you're going to learn and where you want to go. That's a very different set of negotiation calculations. If you're already burdened with family responsibilities and a mortgage and whatever, it's harder to do this. But if you're a single vet, the world is your oyster. Go figure out where you want to go. If you find the right situation, offer to work for free for a while, or at an extremely reduced salary. That's how I got my first job.

"I had been hired as an electronics lab technician at a start-up in Silicon Valley. I quit my job and drove across the country from Michigan. When I showed up for work, I found out they'd fired the guy who'd made me the offer, and the job offer was invalid. I must have looked sad to the people in HR. They said, 'Well, we're hiring training instructors, but obviously that's not you.' I said, 'Oh, I could be a training instructor, too. Just let me talk to the training department manager. When I got in front of him I said, 'Look, you already offered me the job at a lab technician's salary.' I found out they were desperate for an instructor. They had a class to teach in six weeks for the Army Security Agency. They had ten weeks of material, and no one on hand. I said, 'I can do this; here's what I did in the military; I know who your customers are. Just pay me my lab technician's salary.' And they hired me.

The people sitting around the table were fascinated with this story. The woman from the navy said, "Really? That's incredible. I have to remember that story the next time I apply for a job. Then what happened?"

"I did great and, of course, asked for my raise to what they would have paid an actual training instructor. Which was literally a three-times step up, but it wasn't like I asked for it going in. It wasn't like I made this opportunity; this opportunity was there. The most logical thing to do would have been to leave once they told me the job wasn't there. Instead, I remember saying 'I'm not leaving this office until I talk to the head of the training department.' I think the HR people were starting to panic, so they threw me up to the new manager of training and education.

"While it was thirty-five years ago, I still remember that moment. They got on the phone, and called the guys and said meet with him, he might be useful. I was able to convince them I was much better than nothing. Although they didn't understand how much better until ten weeks later."

Noah asked, "So, Steve, even though you had no experience as an instructor, what made you think you could actually do the job?"

"The truth is, this is part of what differentiates an entrepreneur from everyone else. I instinctually knew this was in my competency level, and even though I wasn't a training instructor, I knew I could figure it out. It wasn't just ego; this is where my military training came into play. I had taken enough electronics classes in the military to get a feel of what good and bad teaching was, and I had fixed enough complex equipment to be able to put myself in the shoes of the students. Though in reality I had no idea how complicated the equipment I was about to teach was. It was maybe ten times more complicated than what I had worked on in the military. But I realized the worst they could do was fire me. That you couldn't die if you failed. But I was still good enough to figure it out and got rave reviews as a first-time instructor, which was amazing. I still think about it and laugh."

By this point, everyone around the table had read Steve's short bio in the program. Ricky surreptitiously looked at Steve's Wikipedia biography and discovered he was sitting with one of the pioneers of the tech industry, and he didn't look that old at all! *Man this dude was there at the very beginning,* he thought.

"So that was way back in the seventies, right?" Noah said. "That was a great job. Why'd you quit?"

"I saw a couple of things that opened my eyes. This company was working on projects that were the core of national reconnaissance in the Cold War. These projects were so large, I was just a cog in a very big machine. Not even a cog—probably a small piece.

"Meanwhile, I had friends who were working for these things called 'start-ups.' While the stuff they were working on was laughable compared to the stuff I was working on in terms of technology, I realized they were masters of their own fate, while I was just an employee. To me, their stuff looked a lot more exciting because they could decide what they wanted to do and how they wanted to do it. This start-up stuff sounded exciting, and I wanted to get in the game. So I did."

"So you cofounded a company at that point?" Noah inquired.

"Not at that point. It was another apprenticeship. I took a job in training and, to make a long story short, ended up as manager of the training and education department within three months. The guy who hired me got fired from this company as well. It was like the red shirt guys from *Star Trek*. I mean, they were all dying before I would show up. It was a chip company called Zilog, one of the first microprocessor companies to compete with Intel.

"I ended up teaching microprocessor design, which I knew nothing about when I started., Six weeks later, I was teaching it. And because I knew about the customers and the products, when the company had a job opening about a year into my tenure for someone in product marketing, I looked into it. The opening read 'MBA and five years' experience,' so I applied.

"But they said, 'Steve, you don't even have a college degree.' I said, 'Yeah, but I know the customers better than you do,' and it worked. I got my first marketing job because I had been teaching customers and I understood what they needed, how our product worked, and how to use it to solve customer problems. The rest is history."

Noah was captivated listening to a true innovator. It was as if Steve was knocking down all the psychological barriers holding Noah back. "Wow, that's awesome, Steve," he said. "So I'm seeing a pattern. Everyone who hired you was fired before you showed up! You taught two training classes that you didn't know how to teach until you got there, right?"

Steve laughed and replied, "Yep. That's about right."

Then Ricky chimed in, "So, then you applied for a job that required an MBA and five years' marketing experience, and you had neither, yet you got the job?"

"Yep, and to tell you the truth, I was pretty good at it."

"But that sort of defies logic, or at least the way companies seem to act these days. Why do you think you succeeded at it?" Noah asked.

"Because what I found was that the requirements were completely arbitrary. They didn't even understand what the requirements were. The requirements were a deep understanding of technology and customers. I had both. I knew more about that than most of the marketing department did.

"Then the next job was another start-up in a workstation business. I knew nothing about workstations, but I knew about microprocessors. In fact, before interviewing at my next company I got a call from a recruiter who said something like, 'Your background is perfect—microprocessors, marketing, blah, blah, blah. Why don't you apply? Send me your resume.' So, I sent him my resume. He said, 'Steve, you left out the education part.' I remember that exact moment, because it could have screwed me up forever. I said, 'Well, I didn't go to college.' He said, 'Well, just lie. Put something down.' Remember, this was pre-Internet. There's no way anybody would have found out about it—until now, right? And then everybody would have found out. So we argued for a while. I said, 'Well, I'll think of something. And I did."

"So what did you do then?" Ricky asked.

"Well, I got the interview. The acting VP of sales and marketing was a former computer science professor from Harvard. He looked at my resume and said, 'This box that says education, it's empty. Where the hell did you go to school?' I said, 'Well, I didn't.' He said, 'It says you're a Mensa member. Why did you put down Mensa member?' I said, 'Because I figured the only way you'd invite me in for an interview was if I could let you know how smart I was before you threw the resume in the trash!" It was the only time I ever put Mensa on my resume. The recruiter wanted me to lie and I wouldn't, so I put some proxy for 'I'm intelligent.' It was the only time I ever did that.

"The guy, who, by the way, became one of my mentors, gave me the toughest interview I've ever had. He made me describe in detail what I did, and then turned it around and said "Teach me," and asked some really detailed questions. Holy crap! He said, 'Oh, you worked for Zilog? Great! Take me through the internal architecture of the chip.' I said, 'Okay, I can kind of do that," and then he asked, 'Well, how would you program that?' I'm not really a programmer, but I had taught plenty of companies how to do that. I still remember I was sweating. It wasn't 'tell me about your job history' or the usual interview stuff. It was like a whiteboard interview—which, by the way, is probably the best way to interview someone."

Noah was sweating bullets just thinking about being interviewed by someone like Steve Blank. He asked, "But you got the job?"

"Yeah, I got the job and ended up in that company, four years later, as the VP of marketing, learning stuff I didn't know, but neither did they. I mean, we were making it up as we went along. We had a bunch of smart people. The rest of my career was kind of like that as an entrepreneur."

Everyone at the table was leaning in to hear. The chatter in the room had risen to a high pitch, and dishes clattered as waiters busily cleared the tables now that dinner was drawing to a close. The ex-navy woman on the other side of the table asked, "So what do you say to the young airman, sailor, soldier, or marine who looks at a job posting and says, 'I think I could do this, but I don't have the qualifications'?"

"You've got to decide whether you want a job and a great career or can invent your own. As John Boyd said, 'Do you want to "be" or do you want to "do"?' You can be a title in a company, get along, get promoted, and have a great career. Or do you want to do something—not caring about titles or promotions or even pay?

"Entrepreneurship isn't a job; it's a calling. You don't become an entrepreneur for the title. So if you think a job ends at five and you lust for the security of a paycheck, then you may not want to be an entrepreneur. But if you're doing it because you couldn't imagine doing anything better 24/7, then that's the distinction.

"Entrepreneurs are entrepreneurs 24/7. There is no 'job.'" Steve started to laugh. "By the way, I consider such people small subsets of the population. These are crazy people. These are not normal people. They're much closer to artists than they are to accountants. That's my distinction."

Someone came over to the table and informed Steve they were starting the presentations in a few minutes. Noah had something he was truly curious about and asked, "Steve did you know from the start that you wanted to be an entrepreneur?"

"I knew because I had already worked in Ann Arbor in what turned out to be a start-up, although I didn't know it was called that. I loved it. Everybody else would go home, and I would still be there. I realized decades later that that was the DNA I had, and have had, for my entire life."

A woman who had been sitting across from Steve, but had been quiet thus far, said, "Steve, I'm married with kids, and I've already started my own company. I'd have to say

I'm one of those crazy people because I love my work. I read an interview where you talk about your rules for keeping a family and a start-up. That's something my husband and I talk about all the time. How do you create a business and not mess up your home life?"

"That's really important. I had seen guys who had focused on the business 24/7, operating like a family wasn't even on the list, or was somewhere down on the list, and their kids hated them when they grew up. I decided that was not what I wanted to do. You know the saddest thing is getting rich and being alone, right? That just means you really screwed it up. The truth is my advantage was that my wife had done two start-ups—Apple and then a much smaller start-up. So she knew what the start-up life was about.

"We decided our kids should come home to a parent. So we figured out this set of rules, which I wrote about. You can Google them at 'Epitaph for an Entrepreneur.'"

Noah decided to slip in one last question. "I know you have to go, Steve, but are you saying you think veterans make good entrepreneurs—that what you learned in the military helped prepare you to be an entrepreneur?"

"I learned a sense of responsibility. I learned to hustle and be creative. I learned that in a war zone you could take as much responsibility as you wanted. This was the first time someone had entrusted me with a sharp object and they trusted me with millions of dollars of equipment. Because of the stuff we were working on, in Southeast Asia, I understood if our equipment didn't work, somebody was going to die.

"It was much more responsibility than a nineteen-year-old civilian would get. And finally the military prepared me for dealing with huge bureaucracies and how to go through them like a knife through butter."

Everyone around the table broke out in laughter as Steve excused himself, stood up, and shook hands all around—and then headed to the stage to deliver a talk about innovation and entrepreneurship that transfixed the entire room.

Chapter 12

Back to Bragg

*"All great change in America
begins at the dinner table."*
—Ronald Reagan

The headquarters of the Lorson Office Cleaning Corporation were located in downtown Newark, New Jersey. Monica had only visited the office on rare occasions. The first time was for her initial interview, and then she had attended a few training classes. Just last month the company had held a party to celebrate the start of a new year that was expected to be very successful. At the party, she'd had the opportunity to sit down for a chat with her manager, Lorraine Bradley, and was delighted to learn they shared an interest and background in the military. It turned out that Lorraine was a distant relative of General Omar Bradley, one of the most decorated generals in World War II, and that Lorraine's father and brother had both served in the 82nd.

As Monica explained her responsibilities as a medevac officer, she could see Lorraine's eyes light up with interest.

"You mean to say that you would fly out to the battlefield, and rescue soldiers who were wounded? Weren't you concerned the enemy might still be in the vicinity and that you, too, could get hurt?" Lorraine had asked.

Monica was always surprised at how naïve civilians were about the realities of war. "We always knew that was a distinct possibility. Of course we tried to clear the area in advance, but sometimes that wasn't possible, and we'd have to go in despite, or probably because of, the fact our soldiers were still under fire."

"Well, that sounds very dangerous." Lorraine responded.

Monica thought back to the day she jumped out of the Black Hawk, was advised the field was all clear, and told SueHop to bring out the stretcher. Those were the last words she had ever spoken to her friend. She gathered herself and said, "It was the most dangerous thing I've ever done in my life. We lost a lot of soldiers that way, but that was our job, and we had to do it."

Monica then shifted the conversation to more pleasant topics. SueHop's death was a memory she did not want to revisit. She could rarely go there without feeling waves of guilt, so much so that she felt physically ill. Instead, she commented on how generous it was of the company to throw the party and to give gift certificates to all members of the cleaning staff. She knew that sometimes people could appear insensitive when asking questions about war, but most of the time they were genuinely curious.

That night Monica had looked like any other attractive young woman to Lorraine Bradley. It was impossible for her to imagine Monica in the throes of a gritty, bloody battle. She had gained a new respect for Monica that evening, which was why she had asked Monica to meet with her at the main office on this February morning.

However, Monica had no way of knowing that, and was concerned that she had been called into the office because she was about to be fired. There was always the possibility of cutbacks in the ranks of the cleaning people, particularly if a contract was lost, which happened frequently in this economy. The specter of eminent layoffs was the rumor that regularly circulated among the cleaning staff. Bad news seemed always to be just around the corner and a sense of hopelessness prevailed. Despite the fact that Monica was determined to eventually make a career move, she hadn't made any substantial progress on that front, and she relied upon this paycheck. Consequently, she had been rehearsing the argument she would make to Lorraine once she gave her the bad news, in the hope that she would be able to change her mind.

Monica sat in the reception area feeling a little like she was waiting on death row, when Lorraine burst through the glass doors with a wide smile on her face, extended her hand, and greeted her warmly.

"It's so good to see you, Monica! Let's go back to my office," she said as she held open the door. "Can I get you a cup of coffee on this frosty morning?"

"No thanks, Lorraine. I've already had plenty." Monica was anxious to get this over with.

Once they were settled, Lorraine noticed the apprehensive look on Monica's face and said, "Don't worry. I've got good news for you, or at least I hope you will take it as good news."

Monica relaxed and said, "Oh, I'm relieved. I was a little worried you were going to tell me there were going to be some cutbacks, and I was included."

Lorraine looked surprised. "Now why would we do that? You've done an excellent job for us—in fact, probably too good of a job. We've all been very impressed with the care you take, and the fact that you're never absent and usually arrive early. And on top of that, you never call with complaints, which, I have to tell you, is pretty rare. After we talked at the party, and I learned about your military background, it got me thinking. I realized that you have those qualities for a good reason, and you might be able to help us in a different capacity."

Monica could hardly believe her ears. She thought back to some of her conversations with successful veterans over the previous months, particularly with Tracey Jones, and her suggestion that she give her employer her best effort. She had trusted it would pay off at some point, but little did she realize she would start reaping the rewards this soon. She presumed they were going to make her the manager of her cleaning crew. That would give her some additional responsibility, obviously a nice bump in salary, and, while she would still have to do janitorial work, she could feel she was making progress.

"A different capacity, Lorraine? What do you mean?" Monica asked.

"Well, Monica, our biggest challenge is in hiring and retaining people who are reliable. After all, being a janitor isn't the most glamorous job in the world, and yet we have to hire people we can trust to show up on time, and go into our clients' offices, and meet a certain high standard. We need people who won't just work hard, but also are responsible and trustworthy. Frankly, we've had problems at times.

"After speaking with you, it dawned on me that we have a great resource in our veterans, and that we should be hiring more veterans, and, well, that you would make a great recruiter for us.

"Does that sound interesting to you? And, before you say anything, let me add that it will mean that we'll practically double your salary, and your benefits package will be dramatically improved, including a matching 401(k)."

Monica was completely dumbfounded and didn't know what to say. After an awkward silence, Lorraine added,

"And, by the way, your office will be the one next to mine, and you'll share my assistant with me. Do you want to see your office?"

*

The next several months were challenging, busy, and invigorating for Monica. Her new position as manager of veteran relations was exciting and wide-ranging. Lorraine's boss, the president of Lorson, believed hiring vets would not only improve their workforce, but also enhance their image with the public and encourage new business. He was correct on all fronts. It wasn't long before the *Star-Ledger* ran an article on their efforts, featuring Monica in a photo from her active-duty days. Local businesses responded to the idea of working with a company that believed in hiring veterans; the more publicity Monica generated, the more their business grew.

During the next year, she was invited to speak on several panels organized by veterans' groups, the Chamber of Commerce, and other local business organizations. She couldn't believe she was now on the other side of the microphone, and was making a difference. She knew she owed it all to her very fortunate meeting with Tracey Jones and their discussion around a table in a coffee shop. Monica stayed in constant contact with Tracey, who would usually remind her that, as tremendous as her life was now, it was only going to get better. All she needed to do was make the effort, keep a positive attitude, rest assured that every problem has a solution, and most of all, continue to pass it on. So when she was asked to help organize an event for a nonprofit organization at Fort Bragg, for soldiers who would be transitioning out of the military in the near future, she called Tracey and asked her to be one of the speakers. Not only did Tracey agree to participate, she gave her the names of several other veterans whom she thought might speak, focusing on one in particular.

"Monica, have you ever heard of a guy named Nick Palmisciano?"

"No, I haven't. What's his story?"

"Well, he's a West Point grad, a ranger, and a very successful entrepreneur. Check him out online; you'll find some YouTube videos he's in. Aside from everything else, he's funny, irreverent, and a great speaker, and is always doing things in support of vets. He lives down in North Carolina. I think he was stationed at Bragg at one point, so I'll bet he would be willing to speak there if he's available that weekend."

"That's great, Tracey. Do you think you can put us together?" Monica asked.

"I'm already on the case." Monica could hear the clicking of Tracey's keyboard in the background. "I'll send off an e-mail introducing the two of you and you can arrange for a phone call," Tracey replied.

Monica and Nick exchanged a few e-mails. She checked out his site, Ranger Up, and a few of his other sites, and indeed, he seemed to be an excellent candidate to speak at the forum for transitioning vets. He returned a friendly e-mail saying he would be happy to speak with her on the phone so he could fill her in on his background.

"Hi, Nick, this is Monica Brady. How are you?"

"I'm great, Monica. What's going on?

"Well, I'm involved with an organization called American Dream U, and we're a nonprofit that's involved in helping vets who are processing back into civilian life. We hold events at bases around the country, and try to provide real-life information that will help them make the transition."

"That's really important, particularly with how the military is being downsized these days. If you'd like to have me, I'd be happy to attend. The date you mentioned in your e-mail works for me," Nick replied.

"That's great. I think you'd be a wonderful addition. I'm trying to figure out exactly how to structure the event, so it would be helpful if we could talk a little bit about your background, so I could figure out how best to fit you in. Is that okay with you?"

"Sure, Monica, fire away. I've got about a half hour before I have to get to my next appointment."

"Great. So you're a West Point grad, right? What made you decide to go there? From what I can tell, you probably had your pick of universities!"

"I'll be honest. I wasn't thinking about the military or West Point. Not at all. I was actually focused very much on MIT. That was the college I had in my head that I wanted to go to. I took my PSATs and did pretty well. The very first college that sent me anything was West Point. I looked at the brochure and I was like, 'My God, this is cool.' Then I threw it back down on the table.

"My dad, who really doesn't weigh in on very much—he's a big believer in letting us live our lives—just said, 'I really think you ought to check that out. I think that might be a good fit for you.' I picked up the brochure and looked at it some more and decided to schedule a visit. Over the course of a few weeks, I did the 'visit-a-bunch-of-schools thing' in the area. I went to Brown and MIT and all those sorts of schools that were pretty local to where I lived. At all those schools, the basic message over and over again from the faculty, the kids, and the guides was, 'We're the best. Come here and be among the best.'

"Then I visited West Point. I spent a full day with Cadet Hahn, who was a 'plebe.' He was not a great plebe. Not that he was a bad cadet or anything like that, but he was one of the guys who got picked on a lot. He had a real hard day, but through it all, he was determined to do his job. You could tell that even though he should have been miserable, he had a strong sense of accomplishment about it.

"The very last thing I did that day was have a meal with all the upperclassmen and Cadet Hahn. He had to do all the table duties they do at West Point. He got destroyed once again. I'm just sitting there watching the whole thing, taking it in. The upperclassman at the head of the table walks over to me, leans down, and says, 'Look, don't come here for your parents, don't come here because you think it's cool, don't come here because you think it's going to help your future. Only come here if you want to serve your country, because this is the hardest fucking thing you're ever going to do, and it's four years of absolute torture.'

"Right there, I was hooked. I was like, 'I have to go to this place.' I forgot all about the other schools. I applied to them, but they became the secondary focus."

"What about MIT? Didn't you still consider them?" Monica asked.

"After I found out I was accepted to West Point, I got a call back from MIT, saying they were very interested not only in having me interview to come to the school, but also in meeting with their wrestling coach and so forth. I turned that down. Boston University offered me a full ride. I turned that down as well. At that point, I had to test myself at West Point."

Monica knew the feeling. It was typical to hear veterans say "the easy road is not always the best road." "So, Nick," she continued, "most people would look at your experience watching this poor, probably eighteen- or nineteen-year-old plebe at West Point, and would run from that, and you ran toward it instead."

"Yeah, it was maybe the most challenging thing I've done to this day. What was most scary to me was that I did not initially excel at West Point. That was really hard for me to stomach, and, frankly, for all my classmates to stomach as well. I don't know exactly what the makeup is now—but when I was there, 88 percent of all my classmates had been captains of their sports teams in high school. Everyone there was used to being a leader, a stud, good at everything they had done.

"I showed up, and I went to Beast Barracks, which is the West Point version of basic training. I had a real hard time. I just couldn't memorize all the information perfectly. I could do it perfectly in my room, but when I was standing in front of the upperclassmen and they were yelling at me, I screwed up a lot. I had to recite all these things while they basically made fun of me. Anytime they said, 'Palmisciano, hit it,' I had to shout, 'Sir, I'm a wedge, the simplest machine known to man, and I still don't work.'

Monica and Nick erupted in laughter. "Wow," she said. "That sounds awful. But I get it. It sounds a lot like basic. But the preparation works, and winnows out those who aren't going to make it. I know I would have wished I had taken the easier route, with the college kids at MIT or BU."

"Well, it was emotionally daunting, because I had never been bad at anything. Everything I had done, if I wasn't good at first, I worked hard and in short order became at least solid. Then over time I became good. That was what I had done over and over again in my childhood. Then, suddenly there I was, the low man on the totem pole."

Monica was intrigued by this story. She knew Nick would be great at her event. "So you obviously made it and excelled. What happened then?"

"Then I had a really interesting experience. The one thing I was good at was the physical stuff. My roommate in Beast Barracks was a guy by the name of Dave Wimberly. Everybody on the squad thought, 'This guy is the best. He's an absolute stud. Nothing breaks him.' He was a wrestler also, and he was a much better wrestler than I was. Even the things I was good at, he was better at. We did our final PT test for the first half of Beast Barracks. I was a real fast guy and good at push-ups, so I did very well on the test. But I was disappointed because I had run something like a ten-fifty-four two-mile, and I knew I was capable of doing a ten-thirty-eight.

"My squad leader asked how I did. I said, 'I only ran a ten-fifty-two.' I really meant it. I was upset. The one thing Dave wasn't good at was running. When we got back to our room, he was emotional. He said, 'I don't know why you would say that. I work so hard and I'll never get to eleven, never mind into the tens.' It hit me that everyone was having his own challenges. In everyone's head, this was a monumental task. Even though some people showed it more visibly than others, we were all suffering together.

"That was a big realization. With that, I decided to stop being afraid of failing everything, because that's really how it had become. No matter what it was, no matter how miserable it was going to be, I just started volunteering for everything. Over time the fear went away and my performance went way up. By the time basic training was over, and I went to a new company during Reorganization Week, I became one of the best cadets militarily, certainly in my company, for a long period of time. That is, until I got in trouble my sophomore year for standing up to a kid I felt had sold out some of our classmates—but that's a whole other story. The realization that suffering was just part of it, and everyone had his own challenges and demons was huge for me. I guess a light bulb went off, you might say."

"So," Monica said, "The idea behind our American Dream U event is that we're trying to help the attendees figure out their future plans. And many of them are thinking about becoming entrepreneurs. The speakers talk about their military experience, and also their life experience. I know you have an interesting story, being a ranger, a successful entrepreneur, and a father and husband. Were there any lessons you learned at West Point that helped you become an entrepreneur?"

"Not just at West Point, but in the military proper, in ranger school, and all the different military experiences. You realize there are highs and lows, and hoping and waiting for things to change never helps. Even if you have a mountain of tasks to accomplish, and there's no way to get it all done, your only chance is to systematically work through it. That's what you do at West Point. They purposely give you more than you can do, because you have to start making good decisions about what's most critical.

"Nobody gets everything done at West Point. *Nobody.* The valedictorian every year at West Point does not have a 4.0 because it's impossible. You just can't get everything done. That is essential, as you know, in entrepreneurship. I have two thousand great ideas I would love to execute. We have the best plans set up all the time, but something always changes. Opportunities come at the same time and you have to pick one or do one-and-a-half. Sometimes you have to say no to things that would be amazing, but the timing isn't right. Sometimes you say yes to things even though the organization is going to have to kill itself to make it happen, because you know the opportunity won't present itself again.

"You've got to set up a structure for getting things done, and you've got to work more hours than any person should be able to work. You've got to somehow motivate the organization to execute on a ridiculous timeline. All that comes from knowing if you plug away at it, it's going to happen. I think the difference between entrepreneurs who are successful and those who fail is the ability to endure and continue to move forward, even if it's only one step at a time, and that step takes a long time to accomplish. Sometimes it's just painful."

"There's a story I read in *Think and Grow Rich,*" Monica replied, "about a guy who struck gold, and then gave up because he was digging in the wrong direction. Then he sold his stake to one of his workers, who dug in the right direction and made millions. He gave up when he was three feet from gold. I guess sometimes when you're running your own business, things looks dismal. You're out of cash, but that big order, or whatever it is, is just around the corner. You have to keep chugging along."

Nick could relate to that. "Yeah, all the time. I made some mistakes early on. I was helping a few people who were interested in being entrepreneurs. I found myself doing a lot of work for them. I don't do that anymore. It's not because I don't care. It's because I realized I was caring more about their success than they were. It can never be that way. *You* have to carry the share. Putting it in army terms, everybody has a bad day sometimes. You're on a road march, and you need your buddy to come behind you and put his arm underneath your rucksack and help you move forward. But when I also have to take your rucksack, you're no longer in the fight.

"Nobody gave me a road map for how to be successful, but I tried to do it as often as possible. If I hand you a road map and you continually come back and say, 'Oh, this is hard. Can you help with this part?' over and over and over again, you're not an entrepreneur. You need to get a job in corporate America somewhere, because you're either incapable or unwilling to sacrifice enough to get things done. You have to be the one pushing because it never gets easier. It only gets scarier. The more employees you have, the scarier it gets. The bigger the company gets, the more cash flow you need. Nothing gets easier."

Monica remembered something she had read in one of her self-improvement books. "I can't remember where I read this, but I think it's important. There's a difference between being interested and being committed. If you're interested, you'll do what's convenient. If you're committed, you'll do whatever it takes. I think your example of someone coming to you saying, 'Well, I don't know how to . . .'" shows that person is interested but not committed. When one's committed, one finds a way."

"That's right." Nick agreed. "Actually, that's a great way of putting it. I've never heard it put like that. I may steal that from you in the future. It's 100 percent true."

"You're welcome to it!" Monica said.

"You see that in employees, too. The difference between great employees and good employees is you can take good employees and put them in a position they enjoy, and they will do a good job. Great employees will solve any problem, even if they don't know how at the outset. They will hunt down and find the answer, figure it out, and make it happen."

"I think that's a great point to make. So, can you tell me about being a ranger?

"Four years at West Point and then six years in the military. I was a ranger-qualified infantry soldier during that time."

"Okay. Then what did you do when you got out of the military?"

"I went to Duke University."

"So, that was for your master's?"

"Yep. That was for an MBA."

"And how was that experience?"

Nick hesitated for a moment and then replied, "It was okay. Getting out of the military is bittersweet. My motivation was twofold. I didn't want to be a major. If I could've stayed a platoon leader forever and just moved around in different platoons, I would probably still be in the military. I loved working with the guys. I loved being in the thick of it. A lot of people have told me I should've been an NCO. Maybe they're right. I didn't want to be a major. I didn't want to spend the best working years of my life doing staff work. Right now my classmates are finally getting to a position where they're going to be in command again. I've been out since September 2003 now. A decade of not leading troops is not what I was looking for in order to get two more years of doing it, if that makes sense."

"Yeah, for sure." Monica replied. "I was the same way. Was that your main reason for leaving?"

"That was one reason. The second reason was that I really wanted to have children, and my ex-wife—and I agree with her to this day— said 'I'm not going to have children while you're in the military, for obvious reasons.' You know, I can't imagine having to make the sacrifice a lot of my classmates have made, where they're deployed every other year and have missed out on a lot of stuff with their kids."

This last comment hit Monica in the gut. The hardest thing she ever did was walk away from Danny when Justin was just an infant, and head to Afghanistan. It was difficult for her, but Danny also suffered. Fortunately, she made it back to take care of Justin, or where would he have been? "I know what you mean, Nick. I was deployed when my son was six months old. So that's mainly why you left?"

"Those were my two reasons for getting out, but when you hang up the uniform, you really do feel like a part of you has died. Then anytime anything happens—someone's deployed, someone gets killed, a helicopter goes down, someone you know is injured or killed—you feel an immense amount of guilt. Even to this day, when I hear about someone I know being hurt, I look at myself in the mirror as a little less than because I'm no longer doing the job."

Monica knew exactly what Nick was talking about. This was complicated stuff, emotionally. "Boy, Nick, do I know what you mean."

"I was dealing with that at its rawest right after I got out. I left the military and one of my favorite soldiers died. There I was, just arriving at Duke, and my friend William Maher had just been killed. That was real tough. Plus, it was the height of people talking about Iraq. The 2003–2004 time frame was when everyone was an expert on Iraq, the way that today everyone is an expert on Ferguson or immigration. Iraq was the hot-button topic of the day.

"I was sitting around these people and my buddies were overseas fighting these wars, and there were a lot of arrogant people, well, just being assholes. It's easy to look at it now, coming up on forty, and say, 'Twenty-six-year-olds, that's what they do. They talk shit about the world as if they have real-life experience.' At the time, however, it was infuriating. It was frustrating. I felt like these people had no idea what it was like to actually be in a combat zone. It forces you to appreciate the Western lifestyle we get to live, because it's rare in the world to live as well as we do.

"So, my original feeling at Duke was that I was a fish out of water. I'm not insulting the students at Duke. If the students at Duke and West Point were all to take some sort of standardized test, it's possible the Duke kids would beat the West Pointers, maybe. But I've never been anywhere where the people were more capable, as a whole, than at West Point.

"To stay balanced, I volunteered with the Duke ROTC program, the undergrads. That was a great experience. They were really motivated kids. I taught them mixed martial arts and some small unit tactics. They actually became the inspiration for starting Ranger Up, because they had been complaining about not having cool T-shirts. With a printer and some heat transfers, I made some funny shirts and gave them to the kids. They thought they were great ideas. They encouraged me to think about starting a website, and ultimately I did that."

Monica thought that was pretty cool. "So, Nick, you're saying that, when you look back, if you hadn't volunteered to work with the ROTC kids at Duke, Ranger Up might never have happened."

"Yep. It's true."

"That's what I've found, too," Monica said. "Volunteering usually pays off in unexpected ways."

"I would agree with that 100 percent. I'd even take it a step further, and say I have never been disappointed. Even if it was challenging—even if it was financially challenging—

I've never been disappointed with taking my time to help good people. That has always improved my life, no matter what the cost. Is it like that for you as well, Monica?"

"That's certainly what I've found as well in the last year or so. I was sort of sitting on my pity-pot, and then I began reaching out to some vets, and things started to change for the better. Now that I'm in a position to help others, it gets better and better. It's just sort of a never-ending circle. But enough about me, Nick. I gather that after you graduated from Duke, you entered the corporate world. So how did you wind up going full-time with Ranger Up?"

"The truth is I didn't know what I wanted to do. So at the beginning, while I was at Duke, I basically applied for every type of job—investment banking, consulting, and then general management. I wasn't interested in a marketing job, which is somewhat ironic."

"Why is that ironic?" Monica asked.

"Well, because, essentially, what I do now is all related to marketing."

"So, how did that happen?"

"Like so many things, to a degree it happened by chance. I was fortunate to have two experiences, one good, one bad, that were critical to my going the general management route, which was the right direction for me. The first was that my first investment banking interview was with a West Pointer. He was awesome. Frankly, investment banking was the area I knew the least about. I had really pushed myself to prepare for the interviews, but investment banking definitely wasn't my strong suit.

"I did well in the interview, but at the end, we had the most honest conversation I'd ever had. I really think it was because we were both from West Point. He looked at me and said, 'Nick, I think you'd be great at this job. If you want the job, I'm going to give you an offer. But here's what I want you to think about: I'm not sure you want to be an investment banker. I think you should go home and think about it, and consider all the things we talked about, and what this job really entails, and call me by 9 p.m. If you want it, then I will give you the job. If you don't, then I would look elsewhere for a different line of work.'"

"Wow! That's pretty blunt," Monica said. "What did you do?"

"God bless him, because he was 100 percent right. If I had walked out of there without that conversation, and I had been offered the job, I probably would have taken it, because everyone said, 'You really want an investment banking job. That's the job that everybody should get,' and so forth. I called him back two hours later and said, 'Thanks very much, John. I really appreciate it. You're right. I don't want to be an investment banker.'"

"I've seen your videos, Nick, and I have to admit you don't strike me as the investment banker type."

"Thanks. I'll take that as a compliment," Nick replied.

"Definitely. So what was the other experience? The bad one."

"Well, the next area I looked at was consulting. Again, I did pretty well with consulting interviews. I got to the final round of a consulting interview with one of the Big Three. The guy was a senior partner and, for lack of a better term, a real smug dude. He told me he really liked me, but he wasn't going to hire me until next year, because he wanted me to get some real-world experience first. There was so much wrong with that statement: (a) it implied my military experience wasn't 'real-world' experience, (b) he assumed I would just accept the job from him, and (c) he expected I would accept the job from him next year after he was clearly about to reject me this year. The list goes on and on and on.

"That was a snapshot of how the consulting business saw itself, period. Even though I've met a lot of great consultants, on the whole, that sort of attitude, that 'You're lucky to be here' kind of thing, turned me off from wanting to be in big business consulting. I walked away from the other offers because of that interview."

"So what was it that made you decide to join John Deere?"

"At the end of it, what I really like doing is leading a team of motivated people to an objective. That brought me to John Deere. I liked John Deere a lot because, even though I'm from up North, they're a Midwestern-values company. What that basically meant to me was they were a bunch of really nice people who for the most part meant exactly what they said, and there wasn't a ton of politics to deal with. For most of us, it was just a really good place to work. It was as close to a military-style environment—in terms of a meritocracy and people legitimately trying to help one another—as I'd found in the corporate world.

"That's what brought me there, as opposed to a General Electric or something like that.   I got there, and I had a variety of jobs. I moved through the ranks pretty quickly. It was good work, but ultimately my passion wasn't there."

"So, this whole idea of what drives an entrepreneur is something it would be good for you to talk about," Monica replied. "It sounds like something was compelling you."

"Yeah." Nick seemed to be talking to himself for a second. "If I hadn't started Ranger Up, would I have had any issue continuing to work at John Deere? Probably not! I probably would have kept on doing a good job and moved through the organization, and right now I'd be a director or VP somewhere. But with Ranger Up in the background as my hobby, it got all my creativity and passion.

"When I made the decision to leave John Deere, I was managing business development and acquisitions for the commercial and consumer division, which was a couple billion dollars. It was big job. It was a great job for a thirty-year-old to have. Everyone was happy about it except for me. I left for two reasons. First, I knew if I stayed in the company any longer and made more money, then I would forever be trapped at John Deere or some other big corporation. This might sound weird, but I'd found out through the grapevine that I was going to get promoted again. I was going to be offered even more money than I was making. I was already making more money than any thirty-year-old should make. I knew if I took the position, I'd be trapped. That's when I gave my notice. I found out Friday, and I gave my notice on Monday."

Monica let out a hoot. "That's so amazing, Nick. It's the opposite of what most people would do!"

"I know, strange, huh? The other part of it—and this had been eating at me for a while—was that at some point over the last year, I had realized that John Deere wasn't getting my best anymore. The first three years I'd given my best and done a lot of great stuff there. The last year I was still excelling, but I'd get to the office in the morning and look at what I had to do. It was stuff I could get done in an hour or two if I focused, but I'd take the whole day to do it.

"I simply couldn't motivate myself to be aggressive in that job anymore, because I didn't care. Once you stop caring about something, you have two options: you walk away or you become average. It doesn't matter how good you were at one point. We can all become average through complacency. I knew it was time to go. That's what ultimately led me to take the plunge full-time into entrepreneurship."

"That's quite a story, Nick. When we get you down to Bragg, at the American Dream U event, it would be great if you could share that story."

"I'd be happy to, Monica. Anything else you want me to touch on?"

"Yes. These folks are entering a scary, transitional time. What would you say to them about that in general?"

"I think it's important to be aware that when you transition to something new, you have to prepare for things to be uncomfortable. Most of us have a hard time being uncomfortable. That's why I challenge people to try different things and make themselves uncomfortable, no matter what it is. Once you start getting comfortable in nebulous areas, it's easier to succeed at anything."

"And what advice would you give those who are thinking about starting their own businesses?"

"Specifically, if you decide to transition to being an entrepreneur, check your expectations. New entrepreneurs always think their idea is brilliant. They think it's going to work quickly, and they won't have to put in that much money or suffer too much. The reality is that, minus the handful of exceptions where people get rich overnight, for 99 percent of us, success comes through misery and sacrifice. To get where you want to be, it would take twice as much money, three times as much time, and four times the effort you could even imagine in your worst-case scenario. And then, once you get there, you'll find it's not as good as you thought it would be, and you really want to get somewhere else. It's a never-ending push.

"You can't go into entrepreneurship with the intent of working hard for a short period of time, and then reaching this romanticized world where you just sit on a beach and watch the money come in. You have to want the struggle. You have to love the struggle. You have to like making something where there was nothing. That's what you have to love. You can't just love the money. You can't just love the idea of working for yourself, because everyone works for somebody. I may not have a boss, but I work for a customer. The customer is way more vicious than any boss I've ever had."

"That's a powerful and honest message, Nick. I don't want to take up any more of your time. I truly appreciate your help."

"It's really not a problem. I love going back to Bragg. Any excuse to go there is fine with me."

"That's great, Nick. I'll send all the information in a few days."

After Nick and Monica exchanged their final good-byes, she hung up the phone, leaned back in her chair, and spun around to look out the window. The window in *her* office. She could see the skyline of New York City in the distance, the Freedom Tower glimmering in the twilight, and she was reminded of the day she had met Private Novak. That was over eighteen months ago, and her failure still stung. But here she was, doing work that at least would aid those veterans who wanted help. Then she looked down at her hands and realized she had unconsciously been twirling the diamond ring Mac had slipped on her finger just last week. *My,* she thought, *how things have changed.*

Chapter 13

Outside the Wire

*"The truth of the matter is that you always know the
right thing to do. The hard part is doing it.
—General Norman Schwarzkopf*

A fter Steve Blank finished speaking that night, Ricky
looked over at Noah and said, "You know, man, we
just heard something really powerful tonight. He was talking
about some truly amazing stuff. It just makes you realize the
opportunities are tremendous, and there are lots of people
willing to help vets."

"Well, that's true, but Steve also talked about how hard
it is, not just to start something, but to stick with it. The truth
is, I don't have such a great track record of sticking with
things." Noah had uncharacteristically allowed a little bit of
honesty to creep into the conversation.

"You don't stick with stuff for a lot of reasons, though.
You've got to get honest with yourself about some stuff,
same as I do."

"What do you mean?" Noah knew what his friend
meant, but his default position around this topic always was
to deflect it, to make it about anything other than the real
issue. "I've been sticking with our exercise program. Damn,
I'm probably in better shape than I've been in since I
processed out."

"Yeah, well look, I'm no one to brag. I know I've got
issues with losing my temper and stuff, and I've got to get
my ass in gear and figure out what to do with my life. But
you—listen, I'll just say it—you know you've got a drinking
problem, don't you?"

Noah stood up in a huff and said, "Oh, that's bullshit. Just because you're a loser, don't try to bring me down with you." Then he stormed out of the hall.

Ricky gave him a few minutes to cool off, and then went outside and found Noah sitting on a stone wall smoking a cigarette. "I'll take one of those, Gunny." He rarely smoked these days, but rationalized this situation justified breaking his resolve.

Noah looked at the ground and held out the pack while he mumbled something.

"What did you say, Gunny?"

"I said, 'you might be right.' You know, about the drinking. The thing is that it's not like a regular problem."

"Yeah, I know. I get it. You don't get wasted every time you drink. Like tonight. But every time you get into some sort of situation, it's because you got wasted, right?"

"I guess that's true." Noah thought about the fact he had gotten a second DUI. Ricky didn't know about that, but Theresa did. She had been insisting for years that Noah deal with his drinking problem. And Leslie had flat-out left him because she was fed up with his drinking. Her last words were, "Grow up, asshole." He thought about the old saying that went something like: "If everybody says you have bad breath, maybe you have bad breath."

Noah wasn't ready to concede defeat just yet, however. "You know, Rios, you're not exactly a shining example of a model citizen. Didn't you tell me you recently busted the headlights on your neighbor's car?"

"Yeah, but that jerk was parked in my mom's driveway. I warned him, a bunch of times, but he wouldn't listen."

"I get that, but you know you're eventually gonna go over the edge and get yourself into some real trouble."

"So, we both have some shit we have to work on. I have to work on anger and going overboard, and you, man, have to get your drinking under control."

"Okay, Ricky. I get what you're saying. The truth is, it's something I've been thinking about for a long time, and so I guess it's time to deal with it. I have to do something, I just don't know what."

"You know there's lots of help out there for us. We just have to break down and ask for it. I didn't tell you this, Gunny, but after I smashed that dude's headlights, the court ordered me to take some anger-management classes. And then I had to start seeing a therapist."

"No shit? Really? Is he teaching you to be all cuddly and calm and stuff?"

"Actually, 'he' is a 'she,' and, yeah, she has really gotten me to change. To slow down and think about things instead of reacting. Like just now, when you walked out of that place and called me a loser. The old Ricky probably would have exploded."

"So, what did you do, take a deep breath and count to ten?"

"No, I just detached. I realized what you said wasn't about me. It was about you."

"Okay, Dr. Freud, so you've got me figured out. How do I get my drinking under control?"

"Do the same thing I did. Make a decision to get some help. And when you get that help, start by telling the truth, instead of bullshitting everybody, including yourself. And stop feeling sorry for yourself."

That struck a chord with Noah. Frank Shankwitz had said something similar, when he had asked Frank how he had overcome his challenges. The exact quote had stuck with Noah: "Well, I didn't lie down and feel sorry for myself, which you seem to be doing."

Noah knew he had been slipping and sliding, and that he had a tendency to fall into a funk. Things would be going along just fine, and then it seemed he'd do something purposely to sabotage himself. The one good thing he'd done was to connect with Ricky, who was now being honest and trying to help him.

"You know, Rick, this stuff about getting out of the military and going back into civilian life is really confusing. I've been pretty screwed up since I got out."

"I know, man. When you got that DUI, you lucked out. You could have had a head-on collision. What did you do, drive down an exit ramp the wrong way?"

"Yeah, that's what I did." Noah chuckled in an attempt to ease the embarrassment, but it didn't impress his friend.

"Man, you're lucky you didn't kill anybody."

Noah shook his cigarette pack toward Ricky. "You better have another one," he said. "I've got something else to tell you."

"What's that?"

"Two weeks after that, I got another DUI. It wasn't as bad this time. I was passed out behind the wheel in a parking lot outside a bar, but the keys were in the ignition. So the cops nailed me. It looks like I might lose my license for at least six months."

"No shit. When were you planning to tell me about this?"

Noah was silent, and then replied, "I guess when I wouldn't be able to meet up for PT anymore, if I lost my license."

"Well, damn. That's really great," Ricky replied sarcastically. "PT's been the best thing for us. That means a lot to me, Gunny. That's on you, man. You got me going again, and all sorts of good things have started to happen since then. I've been thinking that if it helped us, it could help a lot of other guys, too."

Noah had been thinking about that as well. After hearing Kelly Perdew on the radio, he had purchased a copy of his book, *Take Command.* It had made a real impression on him. One of the ten leadership principles was selfless service. That was the principle that had stuck with him the morning he heard the interview, when he was driving to meet Ricky. The recurring theme he had heard from Frank, Dino, Kelly, and Blayne was some form of service to others. And tonight they'd had the opportunity to listen to a person of Steve Blank's stature share his story. He knew Steve could be anywhere in the world, sitting on the beach in Malibu or someplace, but instead, here he was, giving his time on a Saturday night to help others.

"We've got ex-soldiers blowing their brains out every day, Ricky. To be honest, I started getting together with you because I thought you were a candidate to do the same thing. But I found it helped me as much as you, probably more. We both know something about how hard it is to get back into civilian life, and how much working out together has helped us."

"That's what I mean. I don't want us to stop, if you lose your license. It's not just the exercise part. If I listen to what my therapist says, it's about being able to dump stuff on other people who understand."

"Yeah, that's what Blayne from Team RWB told me. There's a real need for that connection." Noah looked out over the crowd as they were leaving the event. Men and women, who had been through something so unique and special, were talking and quietly helping each other. It wasn't touchy-feely bullshit, it was just basic training all over again. Only this time, it was basic training in living.

Ricky had something he had to say, but he hesitated, because he wasn't sure how Noah would take it. "Hey, you want to know the truth, Gunny?"

"Yeah, I do. What's the truth? You mean like the meaning of life?"

Rios ignored the levity. "The day you called, I had spent that morning thinking about whether I should drive my car into a tree or a telephone pole or something, or go borrow my uncle's revolver. I wasn't thinking about whether or not I should off myself, I was thinking about how to off myself.

"Then you called, and I thought I had gotten rid of you, but you insisted on showing up at my house.

"Then after we went out, you wouldn't give up and made me meet you the next morning. You were the biggest pain in the ass, but . . . I don't want to get all weird on you, dude, but I think you might have saved my life."

Noah looked out over the boats swaying in the darkness of Gig Harbor, and tried to gather himself. He didn't know what to say, so he tried to minimize things.

"I doubt you would have gone all the way, Rick. You were probably just having a bad day."

"No, dude. It wasn't just that day; it had been going on for a while, and I know I'm not alone. My therapist works with a lot of vets. She tells me it's real. She says there's nothing worse than when you can't reach a guy. You know what else?"

"No, what?"

"She says the best thing to do is exercise and be with other soldiers. It beats medication, therapy, anything else. People need to get out and move their asses, and vets need to get together and get into a routine. So we just sort of stumbled on the solution."

"You know, I've been thinking about the same thing," Noah said, "And listening to all these entrepreneurs tonight, I'll bet there's some sort of business that could come from what we've been doing. You know, do well and do good at the same time. Maybe that's something we should do."

"Not maybe, Gunny. That's something we *are* going to do. It's our next mission."

*

As expected, when Noah went to court regarding his second DUI, his license was suspended for six months. However, by that time Ricky and Noah had hatched a plan. Ricky found a job in the Seattle area and moved into Noah's apartment. And Noah followed up on his plan to get his undergraduate degree and was accepted at the University of Washington in the entrepreneurship program. The Post-9/11 GI Bill not only covered his tuition and books, but also provided money for living expenses. He had also found an excellent therapist who was helping him to understand the reasons behind his binge drinking, and that (coupled with having Ricky around to keep an eye on him) helped to rein in the problem.

After the American Dream U event, Ricky had been bitten by the entrepreneurial bug, and was convinced that their PT program could be turned into a business. So he built a website, and invited veterans in the Seattle area to meet up for PT at the local high school at 0600 hours. Much to his surprise, the very next morning, three guys and two women showed up—despite the fact it was pouring rain. Within a week, they were averaging a dozen folks a day, and not just veterans, but regular civilians who lusted for a taste of the military regimen, as well.

Ricky began to post photos and videos. He came up with the clever idea of providing rucksacks of progressively heavier weights that he rented for a few dollars each. No one objected; in fact, practically everyone wanted to keep on raising the bar. The people who were serious about getting into shape didn't mind having to pay a reasonable price; it seemed to improve their personal commitment. So Ricky and Noah continued to tailor a program that borrowed a little of this from seal training and a little of that from ranger training, along with some good old-fashioned boot camp abuse mixed in for good measure.

Before they knew it, they had outgrown the high school (or, rather, were politely asked to leave). They rented a space behind an abandoned warehouse, and converted the field into a rather impressive obstacle course. Fortunately for Ricky and Noah, Noah's sister, Theresa, was able to provide the seed money. By the end of their first year in business, the group was averaging almost one hundred people a day. Ricky quit his day job, and they began to hire other veterans to aid with the training.

The program started to sell itself, because people were beginning to see some dramatic results, and the results weren't all physical. People were reporting they had undergone serious attitude adjustments. Some people carried these results into the workplace, leading to their first corporate customer and bringing the program to that big tech company's campus. Things were moving so quickly, they were getting a little out of control. It was clear they were onto something. Steve Blank had talked about "disruptive innovation," and Ricky and Noah kept that in mind every time they pushed the envelope a little further. They felt that attitude was what had allowed them to break away from a crowded field that appeared to be a little milquetoast in comparison.

Finally Noah developed the business plan, and he and Ricky were ready to go out in search of financing. They asked several entrepreneurs they had met through American Dream U to sit for a trial run. These were some serious players, who were always looking for the next good investment, and would be ruthless in their assessment. The trial run with their advisory board went pretty well. The numbers added up, the company was scalable, they understood the competition, and they could clearly define the attributes that distinguished them. But they ran up against one major obstacle: the name of the company. When they began, they simply called the company PT, which they continued to use, for lack of a better name. But it didn't "have legs," as one of the potential investors pointed out. A less-generous shark said, "It just sucks; you have to change it. It has no balls, no attitude. It doesn't really stand for anything. You'd better change it before you go out on your road show."

Noah was dejected, but Ricky was challenged by the comment.

"You know, Gunny. I think we've got something really special here, and the name is everything. With the right name, we can sell T-shirts and workout clothes, posters, books—maybe even franchise the idea one day. But we have to bust out from the crowd, and once we have the right name, then we have to develop a signature look, a really cool logo. It's gotta be something we can imagine on every street corner and shopping mall." Ricky had vision, but Noah worried his partner might be getting a little ahead of himself. However, even with their lousy name, they were going to turn a small profit that year, and they had only been in business for eighteen months. The reality was that Noah was thinking small, while Ricky was aiming for the fences.

Ricky and Noah spent the next few weeks brainstorming list upon list of potential names, but nothing was working. Just when Noah was starting to believe they would never find the right name for the company, he was the one to stumble across it.

They were sitting together in their local Starbucks, looking at an array of lists. Nothing was really connecting. Every idea they had was either taken or fell flat, and some of their ideas were downright idiotic. However, even Noah had to admit that PT was not going to move the needle for anyone.

"Well, I guess that guy was right. The name doesn't really stand for anything; it's too safe, too secure. It's the difference between being inside the wire and—they stared at each other and said in unison—outside the wire. That's it!" And that's how Outside the Wire: The Extreme Fitness FOB was born.

*

As they say, the rest is history. Noah and Ricky grew the business over the next few years, and eventually expanded into other markets along the Northwest, and subsequently began to franchise the brand. Each location was run by a veteran; the owners preferred to hire other veterans because they found folks without military experience just couldn't relate to the fitness demands that defined the program. And though OTW grew because it pushed the envelope from the physical side, the company also distinguished itself for another reason. Each location had to agree to set aside a room for at least one hour a day that was open to all veterans, whether or not they were paying members of the club.

Noah and Ricky wanted this space to be a place where rank did not matter. Some of the attendees were business leaders; some were out of work or down on their luck for whatever reason. This was a place where men and women who were veterans could come to discuss honestly the things that were happening in their lives, and to network and support one another whenever possible. They adopted a code of trust and honor toward one another. Ricky and Noah decided to name each conference room after various FOBs that had once existed in Iraq and Afghanistan, so the rooms were given titles such as "Fortitude," "Delta," "Normandy," "Wolverine," and "Lightning." The idea was that, at 1800 each night, they provided a safe place for vets to meet in their communities—or, to put it another way, where veterans were "inside the wire."

Epilogue

"Each smallest act of kindness, reverberates across great distances and spans of time—affecting lives unknown to the one whose generous spirit was the source of this good echo."
—Dean Koontz

U nbeknownst to Monica, her kindness and concern had kindled something in Steve Novak that, prior to that day, he had believed would elude him forever; that something was hope. His circle of friends consisted mainly of other homeless people who were steadfast in their belief that life had passed them by and resolute in their mistrust of all institutions. Perhaps life had simply beaten the hope out of them. Because of that, Novak viewed the homeless shelters in New York City as just temporary way stations; places to find an occasional hot meal and perhaps escape the cold when the winters were at their most brutal. But the strict guidelines that prohibited drugs or alcohol on the premises or some other infringement of the rules usually caused Novak to make a choice that would land him back on the street.

Many strangers had tried to help Novak over the years, but, for the most part, they had faded into the dim haze of his memory—that is, except for Monica Brady Macpherson. For some reason, her unique resolve and sheer unwillingness to abandon him clung to him like a constant companion. She wasn't just another nice lady who threw him some spare change. They had something in common. They shared the bond of being former members of the United States Army, which, regardless of all of his other failings, could never be taken away from PFC Steve Novak. Those few years truly had been the best of his life, despite the fact he had lost a leg in battle. He knew from experience that civilians couldn't understand that concept, so he avoided trying to explain how he felt.

It was another busy weekday night at rush hour as Novak wheeled his way down Seventh Avenue in search of a location that looked promising. He operated on the premise that he improved his chances by changing locations on a regular basis. He knew the neighborhood intimately and was always amazed at how rapidly the storefronts changed hands. *Restaurants open and close in a heartbeat around here,* he mused. *The place that was a drugstore last week is a bodega or nail salon this week.* This was important intel; he could never be certain how a store owner would react when he set up camp in a new location.

He noticed a sign announcing the grand opening of a health club and gravitated toward it because of the military motif and name, Outside the Wire. *That looks pretty cool. I wonder what it's all about,* he thought. As a military man, Novak knew the meaning of the phrase, and what it meant to live outside the wire, because that's where he had been living for a long time. But that was all about to change.

Just as he positioned himself to the side of the entrance and began to fish out his cardboard sign and cup, he heard the front door open, and then a tall black man, who appeared to be the owner, approached him. Novak assumed the worst, because that's what he was used to. *Damn! This guy is probably gonna tell me to move. What a drag!*

Instead the man reached out to shake his hand and said, "Hi, how are you doing? Are you here for the meeting?"

"The meeting? No. I'm just resting for a while. Is that okay? I won't stay long." Novak was hoping he could buy a little time.

"Look, I don't mind if you sit out here, but we have a meeting of vets that's due to start in a few minutes, and I'd appreciate it if you would join us. We've got coffee inside, and frankly we could use a fresh face. What's your name?"

"My name? I'm Steve Novak."

"You've got to be kidding me! PFC Novak, of the 4th Infantry Division?"

"Yeah, but how did you know? Do we know each other?"

By this time, Mac had maneuvered behind Novak's chair and was already beginning to wheel Steve toward the entrance.

"No, *we* don't; but you do know my wife—and I'm certain she's going to be thrilled to see you."

Acknowledgments

I've learned that creating a book and developing a program such as American Dream U could never happen without a great team of people too numerous to mention, and to all of you, I am grateful.

I would also like to thank my wife, Jennifer, and our three children, Phillip, Megan, and Joey, for allowing me to spend time away from home as well as our personal financial resources so that I could follow the mission that is so close to my heart.

And, of course, I thank my mom and dad, who have always been supportive and loving throughout my life. My dad isn't here to see the publication of this book, or the success of American Dream U, but I know he is proud of me.

Special thanks to:

LTG Bob Brown, Maj. Gen. Clarence K. K. Chinn, Maj. General Jefforey A. Smith, Col. Adam Rocke, Col. Michail Huerter, Col. Paul Fellinger, Col. Matthew Elledge, Col. Glenn Waters, Col. Michael Henderson, Col. John Morris, CSM Michael Hatfield, Dan Sullivan, Robert Cooper, Eddie Perez, and many others in the military.

The entire team at Nevada Benefits, DriveSafe Mode, and American Dream U who have supported my efforts and keep the ship moving in my absence.

Michael Fragnito for contributing his writing skills and to his son Luke for lending his military knowledge to our book.

Last, but not least, I must thank all the people who allowed me to conduct interviews with them. You were all very generous with your time and knowledge.

Contributors

Steve Blank is a retired eight-time serial entrepreneur-turned-educator and author, who has changed how start-ups are built and how entrepreneurship is taught around the globe. He is the author of the bestselling *The Startup Owner's Manual*, and his earlier seminal work, *The Four Steps to the Epiphany*, is credited with launching the Lean Startup movement. His May 2013 *Harvard Business Review* article on the Lean Startup defined the movement. Steve is widely recognized as a thought leader on start-ups and innovation. His books and blog have redefined how to build successful start-ups; his Lean LaunchPad class, offered at Stanford, Berkeley and Columbia, has redefined how entrepreneurship is taught; and his Innovation Corps class for the National Science Foundation forever changed how the US commercializes science.

Angela Cody-Rouget is the founder and owner of Major Mom. She is one of three certified professional organizers in Arizona, and a certified family manager. Angela spent eighteen years dedicated to serving her country in the US Air Force, and attained the rank of major. Her husband nicknamed her Major Mom after their first child was born. In 2005, she resigned her commission and worked as a corporate sales representative for five years before starting her organizing company in 2006. Angela earned a BA in speech communication at Indiana University and an MBA from University of Colorado. She is a member of the National Association of Professional Organizers (NAPO) and Faithful Organizers, and has served as the president of the board of directors for NAPO-Colorado. When Angela isn't organizing, you might find her hanging out with her children, hiking in the foothills, working on her book, or cooking fabulous meals.

Tracey Jones is an author, speaker, publisher, Air Force veteran, and daughter of the late best-selling author and motivational speaker, Charlie "Tremendous" Jones. Tracey is the president of Tremendous Leadership the premier publisher and provider of personal development material. After graduating from the United States Air Force Academy, Tracey spent twelve years living all over the world and participating in various global deployments. A decorated veteran of the First Gulf and Bosnian Wars, Tracey successfully used her military-honed leadership skills to land increasingly important roles and responsibilities such as project manager in a Fortune 100 semiconductor company, working on cutting-edge technologies with several defense contracting companies. She is the mother of seven rescue pets and the "co-pawthor" of four books: *True Blue Leadership: Top 10 Tricks from the Chief Motivational Hound, From Underdog to Wonder Dog: Top Ten Ways to Lead Your Pack, Saucy Aussie Living: Top 10 Tricks for Getting a Second Leash on Life*, and *Boxcar Indy: A Square Dog in a Round World*. Her latest release, *Beyond Tremendous: Raising the Bar on Life*, was published in June 2015. Tracey's company has donated over $900,000 to local homeless shelters, mission groups, disaster recovery organizations, and scholarship funds. Tracey enjoys the outdoors, biking, traveling, spending time with her pets, and, of course, reading.

Joseph Kopser serves as CEO/founder of RideScout and chair and professor of leadership and strategy at the University of Texas at Austin. He has served in the army for almost twenty years since graduating from West Point in 1993 with a BS in aerospace engineering. He also received an MPA from the Harvard Kennedy School in 2002. Currently, he is a Next Generation Project Texas Fellow at the Strauss Center at UT-Austin with a focus on energy policy as well as a Leadership Austin alum. On January 1, 2013, Joseph joined the board of directors of the CleanTX Foundation.

Nick Palmisciano spent the best and hardest six years of his life as an infantry officer. While there are many poignant moments to look back on during his time in uniform, perhaps the most important in his military career was teaching, choreographing, and performing an inspired dance to the movie *Bring It On* with the mortar platoon for his battalion commander. That day, as he and the men of the mortars let the world know they were "sexy, cute, and popular to boot" he saw a look of loathing in the old man's face that he had never seen before or since. It was glorious. Upon leaving the military, Nick decided to become a grown-up. He applied to and got into a serious school, studied serious things, got a serious job, bought a serious house, and made serious plans. All of that stuff was seriously painful. To stay connected to the community he cared about and to keep himself from being so damn serious, in 2006 he started a little hobby he called "Ranger Up." He seriously loved the hobby and when he found out he was going to get promoted again to an even more serious job, he quit, which everyone told him was seriously stupid. They were probably right because he went into serious debt to keep Ranger Up running, and seriously almost went bankrupt, but things started working out—seriously well. Nick loves his job because he loves the community that he and the rest of the

RU team gets to serve every single day. He also loves bourbon, caffeine, '80s flicks, combat sports, and any combination of those four things.

Kelly Perdew is an entrepreneur, author, veteran, and winner of season two of *The Apprentice*. He is the cofounder and CEO of TargetClose—a "post-click" conversion optimization and decisioning platform that leverages its proprietary technology and advanced analytics to engage customers with the most relevant digital experience. Prior to TargetClose, he was the CEO of Fastpoint Games and president of ProElite.com. After winning the second season of the NBC hit show *The Apprentice*, Kelly served as an executive vice president in the Trump Organization in New York. He was a manager at Deloitte Consulting and served in the US Army as a military intelligence officer and airborne ranger. He is a nationally recognized speaker on leadership, technology, career development and entrepreneurship. He earned a BS from the US Military Academy at West Point, a JD from the UCLA School of Law, and an MBA from the UCLA Anderson School of Management. He is author of *Take Command: 10 Leadership Principles I Learned in the Military and Put to Work for Donald Trump*, and donates a percentage of the royalties to the USO. Kelly has served as a national celebrity spokesperson for Big Brothers and Big Sisters and the National Guard Youth Challenge Program. He received a Presidential Appointment to the President's Council on Civic Participation and Service in 2006 and was reappointed in 2008. He lives in Los Angeles with his wife, Dawn, and twins, Grant and Grace.

Col. Dino Pick is currently the deputy city manager for Plans and Public Works in the city of Monterey, California.

Col. Pick served in the United States Army for more than twenty-six years before retiring in 2014. Col. Pick served as a military intelligence officer for several years before becoming a Middle East foreign area officer (FAO). As an FAO, Col. Pick served in Kuwait, Iraq, and Jordan. He then came to Monterey to serve as the Defense Language Institute's FAO program director, and later, the commander of DLI from 2010 to 2014. Col. Pick also served as a National Security Affairs Fellow at the Hoover Institution at Stanford University from 2009 to 2010. Col. Pick speaks Arabic, Persian-Farsi, Persian-Dari, and Assyrian, and is a graduate of DLI's Arabic Course.

Frank Shankwitz, founder of the Make a Wish Foundation, was raised in northern Arizona, and graduated from Phoenix College in 1970, with continuing education at Arizona Western College and Arizona State University. Following high school, Frank enlisted in the US Air Force, was stationed in England, and received an honorable discharge in 1965. Upon returning home, Frank was employed by Motorola, Inc., for seven years. In 1972, Frank started his career with the Arizona Department of Public Safety, assigned to the Arizona Highway Patrol as a car officer in Yuma, Arizona. In 1975, Frank was transferred to the Phoenix area to be part of a new ten-man motorcycle tactical unit designed for work throughout the state. Frank was one of the primary officers from the Arizona Highway Patrol responsible for granting the "wish" of a seven-year old boy with leukemia, Chris, who wanted to be a Highway Patrol motorcycle officer like his heroes, Ponch and Jon from the television show *CHiPS*. Chris was made the first and only honorary Arizona Highway Patrol officer in the history of the Arizona Highway Patrol. Chris succumbed to his illness a few days later, and was buried with full police honors in Illinois, with Frank leading the police funeral procession. Chris was the inspiration for Frank's idea to start a nonprofit foundation that would let children "make a wish" and have it come true. Frank retired as a homicide detective from the Arizona Department of Public Safety, returned as a sworn reserve detective assigned to the Prescott Police Department Cold Case Homicide Unit, and is the current secretary/member with the Yavapai County Mounted Sheriff's Posse. Frank and his wife, Kitty, continue to reside in Prescott, Arizona.

Blayne Smith is the executive director of Team RWB. Blayne works closely with Team RWB's board members, staff, and volunteer leaders to develop and implement programs that serve veterans across the country. He provides strategic and operational guidance to the organization while building and managing key partnerships. Blayne is a West Point graduate and former Special Forces officer with combat tours in both Iraq and Afghanistan. Upon leaving the military, he worked at Quest Diagnostics while earning his MBA at the University of Florida. Blayne currently resides in Tampa with his two boys and leads the Team RWB Tampa chapter.

Ms. Mary Kennedy Thompson has been the chief operating officer at the Dwyer Group Inc. since August 2015. Prior to that position, she was president of Mr. Rooter Corporation at the Dwyer Group, and served as the Dwyer Group's executive vice president and vice president of international relations. Ms. Thompson, who was a multi-unit franchisee and served as president of national franchisor Cookies by Design, has a wealth of knowledge and experience in the franchising industry. In 1994, she opened her first Cookies by Design franchise in Austin, Texas. She served for eight years in the US Marine Corps. As a logistics officer, she achieved the rank of captain while on active duty and major in the reserves. In her franchising career, she has earned awards for "Top Performer," "Outstanding Customer Service," and a "Master's Award."

Below is a full list of contributors to *Mission Next*.

Interviews with each contributor can be found at www.MissionNextBook.com.

Tom Aiello, Army, President of MARCH Marketing, LLC, www.marchcorp.com

Dan Alarik, Founder of Grunt Style, http://www.gruntstyle.com/

Will Amos, Marine, Veterans List, http://veteranslist.us/

Damien Banjo, Navy, Founder of Banjo, http://ban.jo/

David Bann, Marine, VP, Sales & Business Development at StreetShares, www.streetshares.com/

Jason Barros, Marine, Program Managerat Udacity

Beth Beeson, USMC, CEO at Little Yellow Footprints, http://littleyellowfootprints.com/

Jason Belvill, USAF, CEO & Co-Founder of BodySpec, https://www.body-spec.com/

Bo Bergstrom, Navy, Co-Founder and Chief Operations Officer at Uvize, https://www.uvize.com/

Steve Blank, USAF, K&S Ranch, www.steveblank.com

Kristina Bragdon, Army, Next Dimension Bakery & Gifts, http://www.nextdimensionbakery.com/about-us.html

Omari Broussard, Navy, Director of Training at 10X Defense, http://10xdefense.com/

Lex R. Brown III, Army National Guard, Solutions By Lex, www.lexbusinesssolutions.com/

Brandon C. Bunch, Marine, Founder & CEO of Hire Our Hero, http://www.hireourhero.com/

Matthew Calcagno, Navy, Big Hearts Home Care, http://www.bigheartshomecare.com/index.php

Dave Cass, Navy Veteran, Uvize, https://www.uvize.com/

Timothy Cerniglia, Air Force, Kumon Instructor, http://www.kumon.com/monument/instructor

Angela Cody-Rouget, USAF, CEO of Major Mom, http://www.majormom.biz/

Todd Connor, Navy Veteran, CEO of The Bunker, Cofounder of Flank 5 Academy, http://bunkerlabs.org/

JT Debolt, Navy, CEO of Shift of Momentum Enterprises, http://jtdebolt.com/

Nikkea Devida, USAF, Wrote, recorded, and performs "Sisters Who Serve," http://sisterswhoserve.org/

Tom Eakin, Army Ranger, Success Engineer at BoomLife, https://goboomlife.com/

Bill Elmore, USAF, Owner, Principal and Chief Instigation Officer at M2BA & M2BI, https://www.linkedin.com/in/william-bill-elmore-64a26756

Ron Fugle, Army, Fire and Adjust, http://fireandadjust.com/

Ralph Galati, USAF, Director of Veterans Services at St. Joseph's University, http://www.sju.edu/information/veterans/about-office

Justen Garrity, Air Force, Veteran Compost,
http://www.veterancompost.com/

Richard Gengler, Navy, Founder of Prevail Health
Solutions,
http://vip.pmidigital.com/?p=360#.VoMSZ2SAOkp

Charlie Gilkey, Army, Productive Flourishing,
http://www.productiveflourishing.com/

Dan Greenleaf, USAF, Chairman and Chief Executive
Officer of Home Solutions,
http://www.infusioncare.com/

Matthew "Griff" Griffin, Army Ranger, Combat Flip Flops,
http://www.combatflipflops.com/

Chad Grills, Army Veteran, "AskChad," Author of *Veterans:
Don't Reintegrate, Rebuild America*,
www.LifeLearning.co

Aaron Heizer, Army, Heizer's Custom Leather,
http://heizerscustomleather.com/

Kevin Hermes, Army Veteran, www.kevinkermes.com

Paul Jenkins, Navy, President and Chief Executive Officer
of Veteran Beer Company,
http://www.veteranbeercompany.com/

Brian Jennings, Concussion Care Center,
http://www.concussioncare.com

Tracey Jones, USAF, Author, Entrepreneur,
http://www.tremendoustracey.com/

Joshua Karrasch, Navy, CEO of The Gun Dude,
thegundude.com

Joseph Kopser, Army, CEO of RideScout,
http://www.ridescoutapp.com/

Michael Kothakota, Army, DataTactix, datatactix.com/

Tim Lawson, Marine, Lawson Entertainment,
http://www.lawsonbluegrass.com/

Jennifer L. MacGregor, Army Veteran, Owner of Combat
Veteran Voicewriters, LLC,
http://www.combatveteranvoicewriters.com/

Mike Maher, Navy Veteran, Head of The Bunker,
Philadelphia, Cofounder of Benjamin's Desk,
http://bunkerlabs.org/

Scott Mann, Special Forces, President of Mannup Leader
Development, http://www.mannup.com/

Josh Mantz, Army Veteran, http://www.joshuamantz.com/

Taylor McLemore, Army, Founder and Director of
TechStars Patriot Boot Camp,
http://www.techstars.com/

Anthony Melchiorri, USAF, Host of *Hotel Impossible*,
http://www.travelchannel.com/shows/hotel-impossible

Brandon Montella, Marine, The Way LLC, Business in
Fitness, Training, Boxing
http://www.everygoalhas.com

Tom Morkes, Army, Author and Entrepreneur,
http://tommorkes.com/

PJ Newton, Marine, Founder of Strategic Athlete,
https://strategicathlete.com/about/coaches/

Leah Olszewski, Army, Recruiter for SOF & Intelligence
Professionals at Quiet Professionals, LLC,
QuietProfessionalsLLC.com

Ryan Ottosen, Marine, President of Housing Our Nation's
Veterans, http://ottosenco.com/

Nick Palmisciano, Army, Founder and President of Ranger
Up (Atomschirm Corporation), www.Rangerup.com

Kelly Perdew, Army Ranger, Founder & CEO at
TargetClose, http://www.kellyperdew.com/

Nick Petros, Army, Director of Marketing at RallyPoint
Networks, Inc., www.Rallypoint.com

Jim Pfautz, Navy Veteran, Self Solutions,
http://selfsolutions.com/

Dino Pick, Army, Deputy City Manager, Plans and Public
Works, Monterey, California,
https://www.linkedin.com/in/dino-pick-50597a41

Sharon Pivirotto, Army, Pivirotto Resource Group – 401k
Best Practices Expert,
https://401kbestpractices.com/about-401k-best-
practices/sharon/

Mike Prevou, Army, President of Strategicks - Strategic
Knowledge Solutions, www.strategicks.com/

Chris Rentner, Navy, Quid Financial,
https://www.linkedin.com/in/chrisrentner

Michele Reynolds, Marine, Success Troops,
http://successtroops.com

Ken Rochon, http://theumbrellasyndicate.co/

Lee Rosenberg, Navy, Managing Director at Navigating
Preparedness, http://Navigatingpreparedness.com

Wes Schaeffer, Navy SEAL, The Sales Whisperer,
thesaleswhisperer.com/

Joy Schoffler, Army Reserves, Founder & Principal of
Leverage PR, http://www.leverage-pr.com/

Charmane Sellers, USAF, ALEON Properties, Inc.,
http://aleonpropertiesinc.com/AI/author/trueme79/

Frank Shankwitz, USAF, Cofounder of the Make-A-Wish
Foundation, http://www.wishman1.com/about/

Blayne Smith, Army, Executive Director of Team RWB,
   www.teamrwb.org

Josh Steinman, Navy, Penance Hall,
   http://www.penancehall.com/

Paul Tijerina, Army, Army Master Fitness Trainer &
   Nutritional Therapy Practitioner,
   http://www.paulctijerina.com/

Daniel Tobon, Army, CEO & Founder of Starchup, Inc.,
   https://starchup.com/

William Treseder, Marine, Partner at BMNT Partners,
   Cofounder of NeuBridges,
   http://taskandpurpose.com/author/william-treseder/

Thomas Typinski, Army, Founder & CEO of Peak Physique
   Inc., http://www.peakphysique.biz

Jaime Velez, Army, CEO and Founder of WebForce1
   Corp., https://about.me/jaimevelez

Melissa Washington, Navy Veteran, LinkedIn Expert,
   Career Strategies, www.MelissaWashington.com

Fred Wellman, Army Veteran, ScoutComm - Veteran social
   enterprise, marketing, public relations,
   http://scoutcommsusa.com

Mel West, Navy, Prosperity Logic,
   http://prosperitylogic.com/

Leon Wilde, Navy Veteran, CEO of Textsafe Teens LLC,
   www.drivesafemode.com

Tom Wolfe, Navy Veteran, Career Coach,
   http://www.tomwolfe-careercoach.com/

Resources

American Dream U Free Online Programs

Mission Next – Successful Military Transition Assistant - https://appsto.re/us/nHksab.i

Creating Your Future Today - http://www.americandreamu.org/CreatingYourFutureToday

Mentorship

American Corporate Partners - http://www.acp-usa.org/

Veterans on Wall Street - http://veteransonwallstreet.com/

Business Incubator

The Bunker Labs - http://bunkerlabs.org/

Military Transition Sites

Soldier for Life - https://soldierforlife.army.mil/

Transition GPS - US Navy - http://www.public.navy.mil/bupers-npc/career/transition/Pages/TAP.aspx

Marine for Life Network – MCCS - http://www.usmc-mccs.org/index.cfm/services/career/marine-for-life-network/

Air Force Personnel Center - http://www.afpc.af.mil/lifeandcareer/transition.asp

Transition Assistance Program – US Coast Guard - http://www.uscg.mil/worklife/transition_assistance.asp

DoD Transition Assistance Program - https://www.dodtap.mil/

Veterans Career Transition Program - http://vets.syr.edu/education/employment-programs/

Interviewee Websites

Ranger Up - http://www.rangerup.com/

Major Mom - http://www.majormom.biz/

Make-A-Wish® America - http://wish.org/

Team RWB - http://www.teamrwb.org/

Steve Blank - Entrepreneurship and Conservation - http://steveblank.com/

Kelly Perdew - http://www.kellyperdew.com/

RideScout - http://ridescout.com/

Mary Kennedy Thompson - The Dwyer Group - http://www.dwyergroup.com/about-us/leadership-team/mary-kennedy-thompson/

Tremendous Tracey - http://www.tremendoustracey.com/

Best Partners

Team RWB - http://www.teamrwb.org/

Team Rubicon - http://www.teamrubiconusa.org

Patriot Boot Camp - http://www.patriotbootcamp.org/

Udacity - https://www.udacity.com

VetFran - http://www.vetfran.com/

US Small Business Administration - https://www.sba.gov/

Strategic Coach - www.StrategicCoach.com

Kauffman Foundation - Founders School - http://www.kauffman.org/what-we-do/programs/entrepreneurship/kauffman-founders-school

Creative Live - https://www.creativelive.com/

People

Forrest Griffin- UFC Hall of Famer > https://twitter.com/ForrestGriffin

UJ Ramdas- Intellegantchange.com > http://www.ujramdas.com/

Giovanni- Archelacademy.ca > http://www.archangelacademy2017.com/

Greg S. Reid- Motivational Speaker > http://www.bookgreg.com/

Brian Jennings- Concussion Care Centers > http://www.concussioncare.com/#home2

Coleen McManus- Spartan Races > www.spartan.com

Todd Tzeng- Venture Capitalist > https://www.linkedin.com/in/todd-tzeng-46958

Brian Kurtz- Copy Writer > http://www.briankurtz.me/

David Jensen- Hiring > http://davidleejensen.com/

Erik Kerr- thedrawshop.com > http://thedrawshop.com
Scott Duffy- Keynote Speaker > http://scottduffy.com/
Tamsen Webster- Speaker Trainer >
	http://tamsenwebster.com/
Brian Smith- Founder of UGG Boots >
	http://briansmithspeaker.com/
Anthony Melchiorri- Hotel Impossible >
	http://www.anthonymelchiorri.com/
Scott Mann- Mission America > www.mannup.com
Frank Shankwitz- Make A Wish Foundation >
	http://www.wishman1.com/
Keith Ferrazzi- Greenlight > http://keithferrazzi.com/
James Malinchak- Secret Millionaire, Motivational
	Speaker > http://malinchak.com/
Mark Gross- Oak Gross Technologies >
	http://www.oakgrovetech.com
Clay Hebert- Entrepreneur > http://clayhebert.com/
Greg S. Reid- Motivational Speaker >
	http://www.bookgreg.com/
Mitch Matthews- Keynote Speaker and Best-selling
	Author > http://mitchmatthews.com/
Aaron Ludin- USF Graduate, Sales >
	http://www.cutcoclosinggifts.com
Jim Sheils- Boardmeetings.com >
	https://www.entrepreneur.com
Steve Daar- http://www.convoforgood.org/
Nicholas Kusmich- http://nicholaskusmich.com/
Curtis Lewsey- Founder of AMcards >
	http://www.appreciationmarketing.com/the-
	authors/
Steve Sisler- Agent of Change >
	http://www.stevesisler.org/
John Bates- Speaker of Training >
	http://executivespeakingsuccess.com/
Iian Ferdman- http://satoriprime.com/podcasts/
Todd Herman- Sports Trainer > http://toddherman.me/

Blogs/Podcasts
Tim Ferriss - http://www.fourhourworkweek.com

Omar Zenhom - http://100mba.net/show/
Aubrey Marcus -
    https://www.aubreymarcus.com/category/podcast/
Grant Cardone - http://grantcardonetv.com/podcasts/
Christine Hassler - http://christinehassler.com/blog-archive/
Ari Meisel - Less Doing - http://lessdoing.com/blog-page/
Jordan Harbinger - Art of Charm -
    http://theartofcharm.com/blog/
Dan Sullivan - 10x Talk - http://10xtalk.com
Jayson Gaignard – Mastermind Talks
    http://www.mmtpodcast.com
Ben Greenfield-
    http://www.bengreenfieldfitness.com/podcasts/
Lewis Howes - School of Greatness -
    http://lewishowes.com/blog/
Dorie Clark - http://dorieclark.com/blog/
Simon Sinek - http://blog.startwithwhy.com/
Steve Blank -
    https://businessradio.wharton.upenn.edu/programs/ent
    repreneurs-are-everywhere
Seth Godin - http://www.sethgodin.com/sg/
Ramit Sethi - http://www.iwillteachyoutoberich.com/blog/
Ryan Holiday - http://ryanholiday.net/category/blog/
Jody Hall - http://www.macpresents.com/macro/
Honoree Corder - http://honoreecorder.com/blog/
Charlie Hoehn - http://charliehoehn.com/blog/
Tucker Max - http://tuckermax.me/
Greg McKeown - http://gregmckeown.com/blog/
Alexa VonTobel - http://www.learnvest.com/author/alexa/
Zig Ziglar - http://www.ziglar.com/blog

Mindset/Purpose Videos

Greg McKeown – American Dream U – Presidio of
    Monterey https://vimeo.com/130170298
Philip McKernan – American Dream U – Fort Benning
    https://vimeo.com/126283612

Simon Sinek

https://www.ted.com/talks/simon_sinek_how_great_leaders_inspire_action?language=en

TV Shows (if you must watch TV)

The Profit- CNBC- Marcus Lemonis

Shark Tank- ABC

Silicon Valley- HBO

Made in the USA
Lexington, KY
27 April 2016